Women in Leading Professions in Middle East

WOMEN IN LEADING PROFESSIONS IN MIDDLE EAST

DOLLY SUNNY

SERIALS PUBLICATIONS
New Delhi

First Published–2003

Published by

Head Office : **SERIALS PUBLICATIONS**
4, B.S.S. Hall, Khyber Pass Market,
Civil Lines, Delhi–110054 (India)
Phone: 0091-11-23811659
Fax: 91-11-23812678
E-mail: serials@satyam.net.in

Branch Office : 4830/24, Prahlad Street, Ansari Road,
Darya Ganj, New Delhi-110002 (India)
Phone: 23245225

Printed at : Tarun Offset Printers,

Forward

Macro economic migration in a competitive society like India can pose the bewildering problems for both the planning strategists and for the social activists. Chronic economic dilemmas caused by pervasive poverty, under spread illiteracy and retarded growth take one to a different line, when issues of equity and social stratification are brought to the fore by political fervent. Official concern to the policy makers is the pronounced disparity in opportunity and the marked regional imbalance that cross endemic conflict. These inherent tensions in the political economy give rise to divergent patterns of economic behaviour and one such prominent trend discernible in the past decades has been continued wave of migrations across various regions within the country, particularly from the rural agricultural hinterlands to the bustling industrial metropolises which offer prospects of empowerment to the young and enterprising job seeker. Migration motivated by a search for better quality of life impacts not only the economic profile of the entire environment but also involves the cultural uprooting of the expectant migrant. The complex issues raised by these processes can be gainfully analysed only if the observer has a firm grasp of the economic principles in the world as well as a sympathetic understanding of the sociological and psychological factors that affect migrant behaviour. I am happy that Dr. Mrs Dolly Sunny who graduated in Maths and opted for Economics at Post Graduation level chose the subject of migration from Kerala to Maharashtra for her Doctoral my study that women migrants, particularly the professionally qualified ones remained rooted to their larger families in Kerala and most of their earnings from hard work in adverse conditions went to the care of their parents and siblings with little concerns for their own future security. Many among them remained unmarried for long years in these all-consuming concerns of family loyalties. My strong empathy with these unfortunate victims of social and familial ties took me to Bahrain in the Middle East where a larger number of Indian women are known to have migrated in search of jobs and professions. During the course of my stay in Bahrain, I came in contact with many working women and others who had flocked to the area in search of better employment and shared in their concerns and frustrations, apart from making enquiries about their future plans. The impressions gathered have been brought together in the form of a small volume, which is dedicated to the hardy and committed tribe of working women from India wherever they may be.

DOLLY SUNNY

Preface

It is a sad truth of Indian polity and society that even 50 years after the attainment of independence from a foreign yoke, the Indian nation has not been able to secure for its women citizen a legitimate place of equality in society. Indian women still face a formidable amount of discrimination in public and private life. Gender justice has remained virtually an empty slogan in the statute books and in the activist discourses, both. While women universally suffer various forms of discrimination, in a poor and unequal society like India women are doubly disadvantaged: rate of literacy is very low and economic independence almost non-existent. Women's access to the avenues of paid employment is extremely limited even where they have managed to secure educational and professional scales and worse still, employed have no control over the income earned due to the patriarchal mindset and the stigma attached to single woman and divorcees. The scenario is truly dismal and distressing to any objective observer and the plight of the women struggling against heavy odds is a tragic picture of heroism and unrelieved sufferings in many cases.

In the profile of the suffering women, particularly those of educated and employed once among them has been etched on my conscience ever since I took up a study of 'Migration from Kerala to Maharashtra' which resulted in the preparation of a thesis leading to the award of Ph.D degree by the Mumbai University. It became evident during theses. As she possesses the requisite academic background best suited to the subject and having been a migrant herself, not out of compulsion, but out of choice has brought to bear upon the subject a rare understanding and objectivity. I have had the opportunity to provide her academic pursuit, guidance and support from time to time and I am glad to note that her desire on the subject entitled has already secured recognition in the form of a grant from the ICSSR. Smt Dolly Sunny has persisted with her academic endeavours for a fuller understanding of the issues involved by additionally obtaining a masters degree subsequently form the prestigious IIPS. It is fitting that the useful and perceptive study on migration prepared by Smt. Dr Dolly Sunny is made available for the use of a wider audience in the form of a book and I am sure that the publication will be found stimulating to the general reader and immensely useful for research scholars both in Economics and demography.

Contents

Chapter One

The Kingdom of Bahrain

INTRODUCTION

The word 'Bahrain' means 'two seas' and is a reference to the natural springs of fresh water which are to be found on the Island. Bahrain is located in Middle East and is formed of an archipelago of 35 small islands in the Persian Gulf, East of Saudi Arabia. The Kingdom has an area of 678 sq km, is largely bare and infertile, though many major drainage schemes begun since 1973. The coastline extends to 161 km and the total land area is 3.5 times the size of Washington, DC.

The country entered into a treaty of protection with the United Kingdom in 1861. Though the country acquired independence on 15 August 1971 from United Kingdom, the independence day is celebrated on 16 December. Bahrain got full independence in 2001 after getting back Hawar islands from United Kingdom according to the decisions taken by World Court, Hague.

Demographic Features

According to 1995 estimates, population of Bahrain constituted 5,55, 000 with major ethnic groups such as Arab 73 percent and Iranian 9 percent, with Pakistani and Indian minorities. The population increased to 603,318 as per July 1997 estimates, which includes 221,182 non-nationals owing to increased migration. The population growth rate is estimated to be 2.18 percent per annum. Table 1 represents the age specific population, birth rate, death rate and related demographic aspects of the country as per the 1997 estimates.

Table 1.1

Age	*Details pertaining to population*
0–14 years	31 percent (male 94,330; female 91,532)
15–64 years	66 percent (male 240,496; female 160,662)
65 years and over	3 percent (male 8,375; female 7,923)
Birth rate	23.01 births/1,000 population
Death rate	3.27 deaths/1,000 population
Infant mortality rate	16.4 deaths/1,000 live births.
Total fertility rate	3.04 children born/woman (1997 est.)
Net migration rate	2.07 migrants/1,000 population

Source: Govt of Bahrain, Website

The details pertaining to sex ratio and life expectancy are indicated in table 1. 2, which throw more light on the masculine population of the Kingdom.

Table 1.2

At birth	1.03 males/female
Under 15 years	1.03 males/female
15–64 years	1.5 males/female
65 years and over	1.06 males/female
Total population	1.32 males/female
Life expectancy at birth total population	74.63 years
Male	72.1 years
Female	77.24 years

Source: Govt of Bahrain, Website

The term literate is defined as those who are above 15 years and are able to read and write with a sense of understanding. As per 1993 estimates total literates comes to around 85 percent.

Medical Profile

Bahrain has a modern, comprehensive health system, whose facilities include in-and-outpatient, dental, pediatric, psychiatric and orthopaedic care. Expatriate Government employees are provided with free medical services in the Government hospital and / or health centers. Free services do not include maternity services, cosmetic treatment, dentistry etc.

Salmaniya Medical Complex is the state run hospital with 1000 beds. It is a teaching Hospital attached to Arabian Gulf University with Accident and Emergency facilities, Laboratories, Pharmacies, Radiology and Physiotherapy. The Complex provides most specialties including dental, pediatrics, internal medicine, ophthalmology, obstetrics, gynaecology, ENT and minor and major surgery. Salmaniya Medical Complex also has a Maternity Unit and an Intensive Care Unit.

Primary care in Bahrain is the responsibility of the 19 regional Health Centers. The centers' normal working hours are 7 a.m. to 2:15 p.m.. Saturday to Tuesday and up to 2 p.m. on Wednesday. Expatriate employees should register with the Health Centers of the locality in which they live. In some instances employing Ministry/ Directorate will assign the employee to a specific Health Center. The centers provide general family medical care. Cases that cannot be handled by the Center are referred to Salmaniya Medical Complex.

The medical coverage will be given as per the terms of contract. It is required for this purpose to get a medical file opened for the employee and family at the nearest Health Center.

Literacy and Education

As per 1995 estimates literacy rate is 85 percent. Education and health services are provided free by the government for all nationals. In the early 1990s schools had a total enrollment of about 101,000 pupils. Higher education is provided by the University of Bahrain which was established in 1986 and the Arabian Gulf University established in1980, both in Manama. Till 2002 the rules did not allow the immigrants to educate their children after 18 years.

Military

Military branches includes Army, Navy, Air Force, Coast Guard and Internal Security Forces. The minimum age for recruitment in military is 15 years. The military expenditures was 6.4 percent of GDP as per 1994 estimates.

History

Bahrain first became important as a Portuguese way station on the route to India in the 1600s. During the 17 and 18 centuries it was frequently under Iranian control. In 1783 the Al-Khalifa dynasty established Bahrain as an independent emirate, but it was soon eclipsed by Great Britain's growing influence in the region. Beginning in 1861, the British forced Bahrain to accept a series of treaties giving them control over its external affairs.

Bahrain's significance increased when oil was discovered in the 1930s. The country remained under British control until 1971; since 1973 it has been a constitutional monarchy and has prospered from its oil exports. After the Iranian Shiite revolution in 1979, unrest grew among Bahrain's Shiites, and Iran revived its claim for the islands.

In 1981 Bahrain reportedly foiled an Iranian-inspired plot to foment revolution there; renewed Iranian attempts to de-stabilise Bahrain were reported in the mid-1980s. During the Persian Gulf War, Bahrain served as a base for allied military operations against Iraq. An upsurge of Shiite unrest in the mid-1990s led to renewed tensions with Iran. In early 1997 the government charged more than 80 Shiites with participating in an Iranian-backed plot to overthrow Bahrain's ruling family. In the late 1990s, human rights observers criticised the government for allegedly using power of arbitrary arrest and to suppress the Shiite uprising.

Administrative Pockets and Political Set up

The experimental parliamentary system was established during periods ranging from1973 to 1975. Now a constitutional monarchy governed by the Amir, appoints a Council of Ministers headed by a prime minister.

The administrative pockets are divided into 12 municipalities (manatiq, singular – mintaqah); Al Hadd, Al Manamah, Al Mintaqah al Gharbiyah, Al Mintaqah al Wusta, Al Mintaqah ash Shamaliyah, Al Muharraq, Ar Rifa'wa al Mintaqah al Janubiyah, Jidd Hafs, Madinat Hamad, Madinat 'Isa, Juzur Hawar, Sitrah

All municipalities are administered from Manamah. The legal system is based on Islamic law and English common law.

Bahrain is ruled by the Al-Khalifa family. A constitution, promulgated in 1973, provided for a national assembly, which met for two years and was dissolved in 1975. Administrative functions are performed by a cabinet.

Bahrain is a member of the United Nations, the Arab League, the World Trade Organisation, and the Organisation of the Islamic Conference.

Previously the country was known as the State of Bahrain and on 14 February 2002 a Royal Decree was issued to change the name to Kingdom of Bahrain headed by the King,His Royal Highness Hameed Bin Issa Al Khalifa who was the head of the state.

It can be considered as an initial step of democratization, according to the decree given by the King. It is done on the basis of an opinion poll conducted among people. Nearly 98.4 percent of the people approved of the decision to convert Bahrain into a Kingdom. In order to ensure peoples participation, it was decided to hold elections. It is reported that Bahrain parliamentary system will resemble that of India.

Executive Branch

Chief of state: Amir ISA bin Salman Al Khalifa (since 2 November 1961)

Head of government: Shaikh KHALIFA bin Salman Al Khalifa (since 19 January 1970) who is brother of Prime Minister who was recently awarded a medal of honour by Philippine government.

Cabinet: Cabinet appointed by the Amir

Elections

So far no elections have been conducted though of late it was decided that the Kingdom will attain more democratic form of government by deciding to conduct elections. The Amir is a traditional Arab monarch; prime minister is appointed by him.

Legislative Branch

Unicameral National Assembly was dissolved on 26 August 1975 and legislative powers were assumed by the

Cabinet and appointed Advisory Council established on 16 December 1992.The Judicial branch is High Civil Appeals Court.

Political Pressure Groups and Leaders

Though political parties and leaders of political parties are prohibited, several small, clandestine leftist and Islamic fundamentalist groups are active in the Kingdom. Following the arrest of a popular Shi'a cleric, Shi'a activists created unrest sporadically since late 1994, demanding the return of an elected National Assembly and solution for unemployment prevailing in the Kingdom.

Economy

The economy of Bahrain is based on the petroleum industry and transit trade. Annual production of oil, extracted since the early 1930s, was approximately 15.4 million barrels. Oil refining is also important. Crude petroleum is supplied by a pipeline from Saudi Arabia. Other industries have been developed to offset declining oil reserves. Prominent among these are aluminum smelting and the manufacture of paper products, clothing, and consumer goods. Agriculture has a vital role to play on the irrigated North coast of Bahrain Island. The important agricultural products are dates, fruits, and vegetables. Fishing is locally important.

Gross Domestic Product

During 1930s oil was discovered, providing the backbone for the country's wealth. In Bahrain, petroleum production and processing account for about 60 percent of export receipts, 60 percent of government revenues, and 30 percent of GDP. Economic conditions have fluctuated with the changing fortunes of oil since 1985. For example the Gulf crisis of 1990–91 adversely affected the prices. Highly developed communication and transportation facilities make Bahrain attractive to numerous multinational firms with business in the Gulf. A large share of exports consists of petroleum products made from imported crude. Construction proceeds on several major industrial projects. The Gross Domestic Product as per 1995 estimates was $7.3 billion where as the per capita GDP constituted $12,000. The imports was estimated to be $3.5 billion with 40 percent from Saudi Arabia and 13 percent from United States. The total exports amounted to $4.2 billions. The share of India was 22 percent and that of Japan was 12 percent.

Transportation Facility

There is no railway service in Bahrain while total highways constitute a total of 2,740 km whereas paved roads constitute 2,159 km and unpaved roads 581 km. An efficient public transport system operates in Bahrain connecting its various towns and villages. Fares are based on a flat rate of 50fils. A large number of taxis also play on road and are required to carry commodities at official rates which must be produced on request of the passenger. Car hire services are also offered by several companies. For connecting to the place of work any of these facilities can be used. After obtaining adequate insurance cover, personal vehicle can be used.

There are 3 airports established in 1996 which include two airports with paved runways and one airport with unpaved runways, which comes to a total of 1 1,524 m and 2,437 m respectively.

Employment and Unemployment

Unemployment, especially among the young, and the depletion of both oil and underground water resources are major long-term economic problems. The GDP in real growth rate corresponds to 3 percent as per 1996 estimates. While analysing GDP composition by sectors, it can be seen that, agriculture constitutes 1 percent, industry 38 percent whereas services 61 percent. The total labour force of the country constitutes 1,40,000 which can be divided by occupation as industry and commerce 85 percent, agriculture 5 percent, services 5 percent, government 3 percent and other occupations represent 2 percent of work force.

The unemployment was 15 percent according to 1996 estimates.

Table 1.3 illuminates the number of employed in the working age group. The male and female dependency ratio as well as active work participation ratio can be understood from the table on the basis of 1981 and 1991 censuses.

Natural Resources

Oil available on land and offshore, natural gas, lime and gypsum are important natural resources. Occupations of the people include oil refining, aluminum smelting and ship repairing. The Kingdom is a major center for oil trading, banking, and commerce.

The natural resources constitutes oil, associated and non associated natural gas. The irrigated land amounts to 10 sq km. There are environmental problems such as desertification resulting from the degradation of limited arable land, periods of drought, and dust storms. Coastal degradation in the form of damage to coastlines, coral reefs, and sea vegetation occur as the result of oil spills and other discharges from large tankers, oil refineries, and distribution stations.

No natural fresh water resources are available in the country. Groundwater and sea water are the only sources of water.

Trade Unions

Trade union activities were not allowed in the Kingdom so far. Occurrence of any disputes were referred to labour courts where the government representatives take

Table 1.3

Employed Population (15 Years & Over) By Age Groups, Nationality and Sex in (1981, 1991) Census

	Nationality/Sex Total		*Non-Bahraini*		*Bahraini*		
	Total as Per 1981	*Total as on 1991*	*Total as Per 1981*	*Total as on 1991*	*Total as per 1981*	*Total as on 1991*	
20-24	25,729	23,850	13,120	13,312	12,609	10,538	20-24
25-29	33,637	44,591	22,385	28,175	11,252	16,416	25-29
30-34	23,972	50,069	16,983	35,468	6,989	14,601	30-34
35-39	15,128	38,475	10,641	27,077	4,487	11,398	35-39
40-44	12,039	23,040	7,653	15,565	4,386	7,475	40-44
45-49	8,460	11,951	4,328	7,567	4,132	4,384	45-49
50-54	6,164	7,777	2,483	3,906	3,681	3,871	50-54
55-59	3,645	4,865	1,043	1,752	2,602	3,113	55-59
60-64	2,107	2,504	443	674	1,664	1,830	60-64
65+	1,859	2,179	279	336	1,580	1,843	65+
Total	**137,892**	**212,070**	**80,714**	**134,802**	**57,178**	**77,268**	

Source: Govt of Bahrain, Website

up the role of mediators to settle the matters. The Kingdom granted permission for the functioning of trade unions in 2002.

Localisation Policy

Retrenchment of migrant labour force from the labour market is visible as a part of localisation policy known as Bahrainisation. In most of the government offices employment is given to Bahraini people. Many of those non-Bahraini's who were employed are removed so as to appoint locals.

Pension Salaries

The following table provides an insight into the pension provided by the Kingdom with clear discrimination on the basis of the country of origin.

Table 1.4

Pension Salaries Paid for Pensioners and Beneficiaries - (1995-1999)

Through the pension fund commissioner in 1000,BDs.

Month	*1999*	*1998*	*1997*	*1996*	*1995*
Jan.	1194.2	1014.0	867.9	623.3	539.2
Feb.	1241.3	1034.7	891.8	638.3	549.8
Mar.	1250.1	1040.8	900.1	651.7	551.5
Apr.	1274.8	1045.0	912.6	659.6	555.1
May	1276.0	1049.9	918.9	766.9	559.2
Jun.	1300.9	1056.5	921.8	775.9	563.3
Jul.	1312.1	1063.4	928.8	779.4	568.8
Aug.	1326.3	1073.2	931.9	786.5	577.5
Sep.	1332.1	1088.1	936.3	790.9	585.1
Oct.	1386.5	1135.1	955.3	808.9	602.5
Nov.	1406.7	1144.0	966.1	818.7	609.2
Dec.	1423.3	1148.8	969.4	822.8	610.8
Total	15,724.3	12,893.5	11,100.9	8,922.9	6,872.0

Through the organization for Social Insurance

Month	*1999*	*1998*	*1997*	*1996*	*1995*
Jan.	841.0	678.2	526.4	380.3	253.8
Feb.	869.0	680.7	542.0	411.1	269.2
Mar.	887.0	705.5	549.8	412.1	273.0
Apr.	873.0	695.3	565.1	421.7	285.4
May	880.0	712.4	578.9	419.8	280.2
Jun.	887.0	713.3	588.8	431.6	283.9
Jul.	891.0	817.3	606.8	434.9	288.0
Aug.	900.0	823.1	622.5	460.3	295.6
Sep.	917.0	838.9	632.0	463.7	300.6
Oct.	915.0	832.0	643.3	460.3	288.2
Nov.	931.0	828.4	658.0	480.4	354.5
Dec.	934.0	872.8	665.2	491.2	373.9
Total	**10,725.0**	**9,197.9**	**7,178.7**	**5,267.4**	**3,546.3**

Source: Govt of Bahrain, Website

While Bahrainis are paid pensions non-Bahrainis are not eligible for pension after retirement. As a result after working in the kingdom for some years non-Bahrainis come back to home countries and settle. Though the table provides data varying from 1995 to 1999, it does not give any break up on the basis of gender.

Industries

The Kingdom has ten industrial areas and more than 500 industries such as petroleum products, chemicals, leather, plastics, clothes, paper, fisheries and food products. Bahrain is a country well known for pearls. Oil industry flourished in the Kingdom after the oil deposits were found in Bahrain for the first time.

Tourism

Bahrain flourished basically due to the measures undertaken in the field of tourism to earn maximum foreign exchange. When the oil resources become scarce, in the long run the country will face problems. Realising this the Kingdom has devised various policies to promote tourism which has drawn world wide attention. Shallack is one of the major tourist spot. In order to attract tourists from all over the world, the hotel industry is flourishing in the Kingdom, creating a lot of employment opportunities.

Telecommunications

Bahrain has an excellent internal and external communications system operated by Bahrain Telecommunications Company popularly known as Batelco. International Direct Dial Service is available to many destinations. Charging commences immediately the called number answers and ceased automatically when the receiver is replaced. For dialing codes of different countries the Telephone Directory can be referred to or 151 may be called for assistance. Concessional rates for telephone calls apply from 7p.m. to 7a.m. daily and on Fridays,, Eid and National Holidays, whole day concession is available. In the absence of residential telephone any one is free to visit Batelco counter nearest to their residence for International Telephone, telex, telegram and fax.

Postal Services

The general post office is located opposite Bab Al Bahrain near Regency Inter Continental Hotel. There are post offices at other different locations in Bahrain such as Muharraq, East Riffa, Adliya, Isa Town, Diplomatic Area etc. These branches are all open from 0700 hours to 1300 hours. The Manamah Post Office is open from 0700 hours to 1930 hours during the working days. Some of the post offices such as Muharraq, Adliya and Isa Town are also open in the evenings on certain fixed days.

The charges for postage in outgoing mail are as follows:

GCC countries: 80 Fils for each ten grams;

Other Arab countries: 85 Fils for each ten grams;

Europe, India, Pakistan and Sri Lanka: 200 Fils for each ten grams;

Far East, Japan, Africa and Australia: 250 Fils for each ten grams;

North and South America and Canada: 250 Fils for each ten grams.

A war fee stamp of 5 Fils has to be attached on each letter. For registered mail additional 500 Fils stamps (for each ten grams) are required to be affixed.

Taxes and Currency

There is no personal income-tax levied in Bahrain. There is also no sales tax or value added tax. The currency applicable in Bahrain is the Bahraini Dinar which is convertible to all currencies, It is divided into 1000 Fils.

The currency notes which are currently in circulation are in the following denominations: 500Fils (brown), BD.1 (red), BD.5 (blue), BD 10 (green) and BD. 20 (Purple and brown). There are also coins of 5, 10, 25, 50 and 100 Fils.

The approximate exchange rate indicates: US \$1=BD.0.377. The Bahraini Dinar, Saudi/Qatari Riyal and UAE Dirham are fixed partly for small transactions i.e. BD.1=QR10=SR10=Dh.10.

There are no restrictions on the import or export of currency and gold.

Religion

Bahrain is a Muslim nation and all are expected to respect this religion. During the month of Ramadan, drinking, smoking and eating in public are not allowed at daylight hours. The immigrants have freedom to have faith in any religion. There are many churches and temples in the Kingdom unlike many Muslim countries. In short, the Kingdom is secular in nature as it does not prohibit immigrants from following their own religion.

Passports, Visas and Residence Permits

Passports are essential to emigrate to Bahrain. After signing a contract to work for the State of Bahrain, passport number, the date and place of issue and the date and place of birth of the migrant should be submitted to the Civil Service Bureau. Those on a married status contract, will also have to submit the names and passport details of the accompanying family members. The Civil Service Bureau uses this information to secure entrance visas called a "No Objection Certificate" or NOC which usually takes a maximum of three weeks to process.

Holder of a British Passport or a passport of a Gulf member state, do not require an entrance visa. After arriving in Bahrain, the Civil Service Bureau arranges residence permits, valid for the term of the contract of the immigrant. For those who are on married status contract, family residence permits are issued to family members also. These permits are stamped "not allowed to work".

During the stay at Bahrain, if renewal of passport or resident permit is required, it should be done one month in advance.

Catering Services

There are a number of popular cafeterias restaurants, coffee shops and Snack bars in the towns. The standards of food handling and preservation are good in Bahrain. Also foods of varied tastes and cultures are available. Given the cosmopolitan nature of society, one will probably find a greater variety of food stuffs readily available when compared to home town.

Driving Licenses And Regulations

Driving in Bahrain is on the left hand side. While driving seat belts are to be used by driver as well as all the passengers. Licenses are issued on personal application to the Traffic and Licensing Directorate, located at South Isa Town. International driving permits are also issued to drivers with two years experience and having a license recognised by the State of Bahrain. Holders of an international driving permit obtained abroad should be re-endorsed by the Directorate before use.

Licenses issued by UK, USA,GCC, are valid in Bahrain without necessary endorsement. Indian license holders need to secure new license from the Kingdom of Bahrain. For obtaining driving license, training can be acquired through an authorized instructor at the rate of BD.3/- per hour. On acquiring the desired skill and competence, the instructor arranges for driving test.

Banking Facilities

The banking and financial services in Bahrain are provided through a number of commercial banks. Those who are employed with Ministry of Health can open an account with the Bank. The salary is normally paid in Bank Account every month. A pass book and cheque book are issued on request. Money can be drawn either through ATM (Automatic Teller Machine) or through withdrawal slips and cheques from any branch of National Bank of Bahrain.

Laundry Services

Most of the residential areas have laundry or dry cleaner shops where one can get the desired service within 24 hours.

Shopping Facility

Every residential area has self contained stores where one can buy normal provisions such as packed food stuff, meat, vegetables, fruits, toilet and sanitary materials, cosmetics and any other normal requirements. Some areas have got larger Departmental Stores where a wide variety of items are available. The largest shopping center is in Central Market where practically everything is available under one roof.

Social Life And Entertainment Centers

Bahrain is very multi cultured and there are no social distinctions in housing, schooling, work or other areas. There are a number of International and Regional clubs in Bahrain and in course of time any one can have the membership of the Clubs of ones choice. The Cinema Theaters in Bahrain are listed below in table 1.4.

Table 1.4

Prominent Theatres

Name of the Theatre	*Location*	*Tel. No.*
Al-Jazeera	Muharraq	258204
Al-Nasar	Manama	258233
Al-Hamra	Manama	258203
Andalus	Isa Town	258202
Awal Cinema	Manama	272804
Delmon	Awali	258205
Muharraq	Muharraq	320823

Source: Govt of Bahrain, Website

Some of the popular gardens and public parks are Water Gardens, Salmaniya Gardens, Andalus Garden, Budaiya Garden, Zallaq Beach, Al-Jazayer Beach, Al-Wasmeyah Beach, Adhari Park and Al-Areen Wild Life Park.

Begging

Begging is banned in the Kingdom as unemployed Bahraini's are provided with hefty unemployment allowance. Police takes frequent rounds to ensure that there are no beggars at public places. Bahrain is a country that generously assists individuals during various emergencies as indicated in Table 1.5

The social welfare measures provided by the state by detailing the amount of assistance, total number of families covered and the number of individuals who are the beneficiaries of the individual payments are separately shown in the table 1.5. Welfare measures are undertaken in various heads such as disability, senility, sickness, widowhood of women, and divorce. While carefully going through the various items it is clear that these measures are basically meant for protecting women who undergo various tragedies in life. The amount of assistance in Bahraini Dinar increased from 3,705,158 in 1995 to 3,881,968 in 1999. The number of families who received assistance was 10,328 and 10,604 respectively for the above years.

The recipients of social welfare while bifurcated into males and females brings to light the fact that women are leading beneficiaries in both 1998 as well as 1999. Permanent care, day care, temporary care, physiotherapy etc. are to name a few. The table 1.6 includes the assistance provided to the Shikhan Al-Faresi Centre for Social Welfare Home, Home of National Bank of Bahrain Welfare of the Aged, Child Care Centre and Muharraq Social Welfare Centre.

Hours of Business

Government Offices commence working from 7:00a.m. and close at 2:15p.m from Saturday to Wednesday.

Table 1.5

Value of Welfare Payments and Number of Recipient Households and Individual According to Reason of Assistance (1995 -1999)

Reason of Assistance	*Year and Value of receipts in BD*				
	1999	*1998*	*1997*	*1996*	*1995*
Disability	236,753	224,933	509,644	507,981	505,857
Senility	1,715,721	1,664,417	1,005,428	1,020,971	1,026,945
Sickness	128,866	105,486	321,073	312,888	304,539
'widowhood (women)	489,357	468,349	717,366	725,513	730,686
Divorce and Celibacy	362,359	335,410	406,405	393,639	387,555
Orphanage	94,608	98,076	55,845	62,102	67,738
Poverty	832,864	781,806	653,281	665,826	667,002
Imprisonment of Bread-Winner	21,440	18,330	16,473	16,238	14,836
Total	**3,881,968**	**3,696,807**	**3,685,515**	**3,705,158**	**3,705,158**

(Table Contd...)

(Table Contd...)

Reason of Assistance	*Year and Value of receipts in BD*				
	1999	*1998*	*1997*	*1996*	*1995*
Number of Families					
Disability	739	727	1,422	1,390	1,388
Senility	4,822	5,013	2,917	2,891	2,922
Sickness	362	281	917	864	833
'widowhood (women)	1,284	1,304	2,030	2,025	2,015
Divorce and Celibacy	1,106	1,043	1,597	1,504	1,452
Orphanage	284	315	178	196	209
Poverty	1,955	1,953	1,444	1,438	1,442
Imprisonment of Bread-Winner	52	45	76	72	67
Total	**10,604**	**10,681**	**10,581**	**10,380**	**10,328**

(Table Contd...)

(Table Contd...)

Reason of Assistance	*Year and Value of receipts in BD*				
	1999	*1998*	*1997*	*1996*	*1995*
Number of Individuals					
Disability	1,434	1,424	4,243	4,367	4,387
Senility	12,261	12,738	10,654	11,540	11,640
Sickness	1,264	1,028	4,024	4,069	3,920
'widowhood (women)	3,970	4,225	3,705	4,198	4,504
Divorce and Celibacy	2,434	2,370	3,049	3,185	3,135
Orphanage	515	634	211	154	215
Poverty	7,987	8,393	6,801	7,595	7,663
Imprisonment of Bread-Winner	223	200	352	359	327
Total	**30,088**	**31,012**	**33,039**	**35,467**	**35,791**

Source: Govt of Bahrain, Website

Table 1.6

Beneficiaries of Social Welfare by Gender (1998–1999)

Item	*1999*			*1998*		
	Total	*Female*	*Male*	*Total*	*Female*	*Male*
Social Rehabilitation	238	112	126	221	103	118
Permanent Care	15	10	5	15	10	5
Temporary Care	11	7	4	7	5	2
Day Care	159	66	93	151	62	89
Physiotherapy	53	29	24	48	26	22
Centre	510	221	289	463	199	264
The Shikhan Al-Faresi Center for Total Communications	136	72	64	134	79	55
Special Education Unit	61	24	37	57	14	43
Vocational Rehabilitation	153	62	91	121	50	71
Bank of Bahrain and Kuwait	160	63	97	151	56	95
'Social Welfare Home						
(Beggars)	**0**	0	0	52	33	19
Childcare Home	36	2	34	38	6	32
Parents Unknown	35	2	33	37	6	31
Children of Broken Families	1	0	1	1	0	1

(Table Contd...)

(Table Contd...)

Item	*1999*			*1998*		
	Total	*Female*	*Male*	*Total*	*Female*	*Male*
Home of National Bank of						
Bahrain Welfare of the Aged	161	88	73	146	75	71
Permanent Care	55	28	27	60	28	32
Temporary Care	1	1	0	0	0	0
Families Care	105	59	46	86	47	39
Child day Care Centre	0	0	0	23	10	13
Muharraq Social						
Welfare Centre	70	30	40	107	49	58
Permanent Care	65	27	38	61	27	34
Intermittent Care	1	0	1	0	0	0
Temporary Care	4	3	1	3	0	3
Day Care	0	0	0	43	22	21
Total	**1,015**	**453**	**562**	**1,050**	**475**	**575**

Source: Govt of Bahrain, Website

Thursday and Friday are holidays. However, all senior staff have to be available for additional working time without payment or a change of working hours to satisfy the organisational needs.

Banks are open from 7:30 a.m. to 12:00noon from Saturday to Thursday so as to enable transactions. Some banks now open during the afternoons as well. Offices under private sector function from 8:00a.m. to 12:30 p.m. and 3:00p.m. to 6:00 p.m. Saturday to Thursday. These timings are not observed by all. Some companies are closed on Thursday afternoons. Business is not usually conducted in the afternoons.

Public Holidays

The dates of Muslim Holidays depend upon lunar sighting, according to the Muslim lunar linked calendar. If any holiday happens to fall on Friday, it is made up on the next day. Roughly speaking the following holidays are observed in the country.

New Year's day: January, 1st.

Eid Al Fitr: Three consecutive days starting from first day of the Eid. (end of Ramadan)

Eid Al Adha: -do- (Feast of the sacrificed)

Islamic New Year: One day

Ashoora: Two days

Mawlid Al Nabi: One day (The Prophet's Birthday)

National Day: December 16th.

Weather

The climate has extreme variations with mild, pleasant winters and very hot, humid summers. The average temperature is 19 degree C in January and in summer it rises to 36 degree C. Humidity is of 97 percent in September.

October-November and April- May are pleasant months in Bahrain. Through out summer which varies between June to September the weather is very hot and humid with mid-day temperatures reaching 44C and humidity exceeding 85 percent. December to March the weather is much cooler, particularly in the evenings, when light weight woolens are needed. The rainfall is scanty and irregular. Gusty winds accompany the rain which is at average 35 mm/1.4 inches.

Language

The official language is Arabic though English, Parsi and Urdu are also spoken.

Official Publications

Official publications pertaining to the country are available at local bookstalls. Some of the booklets providing authentic information about the Kingdom are, "The Islands of Bahrain", "Loking for Dilmun", "Bahrain Ato Z" and "Glimpses of Bahrain from its Past".

Custom Regulations

Those who reach Bahrain from various countries are permitted to bring 400 cigarettes, 50 cigars, 250 gms of tobacco and 8 ounce of perfume. Personal and used goods are allowed to bring free of duty. Import duties are charged on goods including cultured pearls, fire arms, ammunition or any goods restricted by the Middle East countries.

Cases Registered in High and Junior Courts

The details pertaining to various types of cases registered in court reflect the fact that the Kingdom is very strict about the implementation of law and order. Punitive measures are implemented whenever it is required without any favouritism or discrimination.

Table 1.5

Specification of Cases by High and Junior Criminal Courts (1st.Grade)(1998-1999)

Year / Distribution *Year / Distribution of Case*	*Court*				
	Total	*Criminal medium Court*		*Civil High Court*	
		Traffic	*Criminal*	*Criminal Dept.*	
		1998			
Cases carried over from 1997	2,720	381	1,891	448	
New Cases for 1998	10,410	7,617	2,676	117	
Cases transferred from other Courts	17	6	11	0	
Total Cases for 1998	13,147	8,004	4,578	565	1998
Cases cleared	10,901	7,510	3,173	218	
Total Cases accomplished	10,901	7,510	3,173	218	
Remaining Cases from 1998	2,246	494	1,405	347	
Percentage of remaining Cases to the total	17.1	6.2	30.7	61.4	

Source: Govt of Bahrain, Website

Labour Courts

Whenever any employer is kicked out of the job without paying wages or salaries by the management, they can approach labour courts. Most of the times the verdict comes in favour of the employee. However influential people like King, Prince and Minister have important decision making powers in this regard also.

General Organisation for Social Insurance

It is required that those working in Bahrain should submit passports and cpr so as to take insurance policy. Those who meet with accidents can have insurance assistance from them. The insurance premium varies in accordance with salary.

The Nature of Contracts

It is known that basically the contracts are for two years. Only for higher level jobs it can be for 6 months or 1 year. If the employee is found to be hardworking and satisfactory, afterwards the contracts can be renewed for another 2 years. Jobs of permanent nature are very rare here.

It is required that those working in Bahrain should submit passports and cpr so as to take insurance policy. Those who meet with accidents can have insurance assistance from them. The insurance premium varies in accordance with salary.

Chapter Two

Women in Bahrain

Women in Islam

The role assigned to woman in Bahrain is closely associated to the importance given to her in Islam. Islamic faith in relation to women ensures fair degree of equality between men and women in different affairs. In the Holy Quran there are many verses which indicate that the Almighty has created both men and women in the same way and so in the eyes of God both are equal. The Quran stresses that no one should look upon woman as inferior creature. Woman has equal right and is not an object to satisfy the passion of man (Muskrat Johan, 1978). Faros (1990) has concluded that Islam, in principle protects and propagates the religious, economic and political rights of women. As quoted by her, the prophet has said "if a daughter is born to a person and he brings her up, gives her a good education and trains her in the art of life, I shall myself stand between him and hell fire."

According to Kidwai (1978) Islam provides security and right of property to women. Islam introduced the custom of Maher to safeguard the interest of woman after her marriage. Prophet Mohammed made a bold declaration that paradise lies at the feet of mothers. Islam abolished infanticide. It was a step which brought a revolution in the life of women. Islam allows remarriage to the widows.

However, purdah and Shairiat in Muslim law make the Muslim woman suffer adversely. Polygamy is permissible and divorce law is more favorable to men than to woman. Traditional sex roles are adhered to, rather rigidly under Islamic provisions. Muslim woman are not permitted to offer prayers in public or at mosques along with men, nor they are permitted to participated in many sports and services under the Islamic rules. Many service and jobs demanding field work, vigor and strength are reserved for men. Higgins (1985), after studying the position of women in the Islamic Republic of Iran has concluded that political and economic problems have increased pressures on women to adhere to conservative Islamic standards of public morality, codes of conduct and the provisions of the Shari at. These scenes are true for India and elsewhere as well.

Women and NGOs

The process of female labour emigration, of skilled as well as unskilled, to the Middle East Countries in general and Bahrain in particular is a well known fact and is a fascinating subject of study from the economic, sociological and psychological points of view. The female migrant may be used to a tradition of peaceful life in the home country but may suddenly get exposed to a cultural set back in an alien country with altogether different working and living conditions. In the process of migration they may even have to go through many unpleasant situations. The Kingdom of Bahrain has undertaken varied measures in this regard. One among them is to encourage the functioning of Non Governmental Organizations (NGOs).

Today, over four thousand women in Bahrain are members of NGOs and many have taken leading roles. Many women have become office bearers too. For example, Dr Sabeeka Al-Najjar, is the female Secretary General of the country's independent human rights group, the Bahrain Society for Human Rights.

It is observed that millions of young illiterate women from South Asia are compelled to leave home in search of job due to abject poverty. Unfortunately some of them are being sexually exploited and have become exposed to HIV in the process. Most of the 243 million poor women in South Asia have few choices in life including that of choice of sexual partners. The South Asian women's vulnerability to HIV was the topic of discussion at the Fifth International Conference on AIDS in Asia and the Pacific (ICAPP) held in Kuala Lumpur in October 2001. According to Nay Htun, UN assistant Secretary General and UNDP regional director for Asia and the Pacific, poor South Asian women are neither free nor adequately informed to take up secure employment. He further stated that trafficking in women intensifies the problem with illegal migration, making it difficult to ascertain their numbers accurately. According to NGO sources, cited by Nay Htun, there could be as many as 20,000 Nepali girls involved in the sex trade in India while hundreds of Bangladeshi women are illegally transported into Pakistan every day. Governments of the South Asian Association for Regional Cooperation (SAARC) have called for collaborative action to prevent the trafficking of women, after realising the extent and magnitude of the problem.

It should be noted that out of the 1.3 billion people in the world who live on an income of below one dollar a day, South Asia houses 515 million. Poverty, coupled with illiteracy have resulted in depriving people information and control over their lives necessary for protection against HIV. The population of the SAARC nations in general and the population of India, Pakistan, Nepal, Bhutan and Sri Lanka in particular is now becoming the epicentre of the HIV epidemic with five million people already infected. To compound the problem, migrant workers have a negative image in the eyes of host communities and are often blamed for social problems including spreading infectious diseases.

Status of Women in Bahrain

Women in Bahrain have always played a prominent role in society. The first girl's school in the Gulf was established before the Second World War. Today, more women graduate from the country's universities than men. Women are now well represented in the labour force, comprising thirty per cent of the total. However, there still remain obstacles to be tackled, particularly with regard to traditional attitudes, but there is an awareness, both within the government and society, that attitudes need to change if the country is to achieve its full potential.

Ever since independence in 1971, the government has made women's equality, a central tenet of its programme. The reform process initiated by Sheikh Hamad since his accession to the throne in March 1999 has served to promote the position of women in society. Women have not only benefited from the reforms but have been active participants in the process: six of the forty-six members of the Committee that drafted the National Charter of Action were females.

Thanks to the spread of education at a very early age and importance given to education in Bahrain, women got a comparatively better role in the Kingdom among Arab countries. Table 2.1 elaborates this fact.

The Role Played by Government to Improve Women Status

The government of Bahrain has always stressed the importance of defining itself through confronting the issues that face the country and inspired by this approach the Supreme Council for Women was formed in Bahrain. Followed by this, two more non-governmental women's organisations have been formed: the Union of Bahraini Women and the Bahrain Women's Society. The Union of Bahraini Women was formed to coordinate the activities of

Table 2.1

Details pertaining to education

1998/99	*1997/98*	*1996/97*	*Education and Educational Services*
581	577	591	Students Per School (Total)
595	593	605	Government
523	504	524	Private
			Students in Universities, Colleges and Institutes
			Universities
9,665	7,948	6,825	Bahrain University
776	774	781	College of Education
2,207	1,825	1,502	College of Arts
1,426	1,173	1,157	College of Science
3,809	2,709	1,747	College of Business Admin.
1,447	1,467	1,638	College of Engineering
569	557	536	Arabian Gulf University
423	395	375	College of Medicine
146	162	161	College of Graduates
1,174	1,598	1,584	Abroad
			Colleges and Institutes
4,999	4,538	3,560	Bahrain Training Institute
610	696	637	College of Health Sciences
4,098	3,335	3,112	Batelco Training Centre *
204	202	125	Gulf Hospitality and Tourism College
56	62	70	Saudi Bahraini Institute for the Blind
3,877	3,957	3,892	Adult Education Centres

- Includes Students in Short Co
- urses Also at Batelco Training Centre.

Source: Govt of Bahrain, Website

existing women's and families' groups. The formation of the Union will allow a higher degree of coordination among women's groups and provide them with an opportunity to put forward their agenda with more emphasis. The Bahrain Women's Society on the other hand is a campaigning body which aims to create awareness of women's legal rights, as well as other issues that affect women, such as globalisation, information technology, the environment, healthcare, culture, the family and living in a multicultural society. The Society intends to offer training for women in legal rights, non-traditional career opportunities and environmental issues. Issues which affect women's daily lives, such as health awareness in rural areas, will also be addressed by the society.

Economic empowerment is achieved to strengthen women's economic rights and empower them to enjoy secure livelihoods. The attainment of Women's Human Rights are aimed at eliminating all forms of violence against women and transform development into a more peaceful, equitable and sustainable process. Various NGOs function within the Kingdom through capacity-building as a tool to gender-mainstreaming and to gender-sensitise decision-making.

The Supreme Council for Women also set up an adhoc committee to spread awareness among voters on the municipal elections and to train nominees on the electoral process and support Bahraini women who plan to contest the municipal elections.

According to Bahrain Tribune (2002), the Kingdom is keen on privatisation and deregulation in the wake of globalisation and on fulfilling its commitments with the World Trade Organisation (WTO) to cut subsidies, as a case study has said. The government strongly believes in privatisation to achieve sustained economic development. There is special campaign arranged to improve public health as per Bahrain Tribune, (2000). The report indicates that boy scouts and girl guides in Bahrain are the target of a special campaign to improve the health status of the population. The level of education seems to have improved at all levels. According to Bahrain Tribune (December 30, 2001) report by quoting the Prime Minister, Shaikh Khalifa bin Salman states that Bahrain is keen to develop and encourage education and has great appreciation for the role of teachers in the community.

The involvement of women is part of the overall national movement distinguished by several activities of various women's sectors. The lead taken by the Kingdom in modernization of education has inspired other Arab countries also to acquire equality with other countries in the Information Technology Sector's Programme in academic institutions kingdom-wide and in encouraging investment in the sector. The main objective is women's economic empowerment through sector-specific interventions, where growing industry sectors are identified as platforms for integrating women into the high end of the work value-chain. The programme takes this gender-equalising initiative one step further to link up the academy graduates with the job market through a job placement programme that will be established in cooperation with the private sector.

Economic Empowerment Programme

The Economic Empowerment Programme is devised to attain women's economic empowerment. It seeks innovative interventions in the marketplace in growth sectors like the Information and Communication Technology, and the Tourism sectors. This new approach builds on the cumulative experience gained through Small and Medium Enterprise Development Programme implemented in the past five years.

Violence Against Women

Advocating Women's Human Rights, the focus shifted from an emphasis on Violence Against Women in 1998 to development on the Convention on the Elimination of all forms of Discrimination Against Women (CEDAW) training and awareness-raising.

Council for women

Bahrain has established a council to promote the role of women in society on the orders of Emir Hamad Bin Issa Al Khalifa. (AFP, 2001).The 14-member council, to be headed by the emir's wife, Sheikh Sabika bin Ibrahim Al Khalifa, will promote women in Bahrain to assume responsibilities and play their role in the community. It will also draw up a national programme to guarantee the end of all forms of discrimination towards women in Bahrain.

Right to Vote

While Bahraini women enjoyed the right to vote, in most of the Gulf monarchies, women still play a secondary role in civic life. The creation of the council comes in the midst of moves led by Bahrain's emir to restore the country's democratic parliament, which was dissolved in 1975, sparking years of civil unrest, within the context of a constitutional monarchy.

Women's Rights

Bahrain is particularly proud of its record with regard to women's rights. Equality is guaranteed by the constitution of 1973. Accordingly, women have equal rights to education, property ownership, housing and health care. The constitution, combined with an international outlook, meant that the country has been receptive to international trends promoting equality between the sexes. Bahrain has a reputation as the most liberal and pluralistic state in the region, and historically it has led the way in the promotion of women - particularly in the field of education. In 1928 Bahrain was the first Gulf country to open a girls school. In 1962, the first adult literacy classes began after a campaign led by women's organisations to promote education for those who missed out on schooling earlier in life. The programme targeted women specifically, and included health awareness classes and information on family planning.

Girls in Higher Education

Today, girls outnumber boys in school: in the academic year 1999-2000, 58,442 girls were enrolled in school, compared to 56,907 boys. Female students also outnumber male students in higher education. The government has sought to ensure that women are equally qualified at postgraduate level. The Kingdom provides financial assistance and scholarships to female students who wish to pursue their post graduate studies abroad. During the 1970s the government set up different panels to integrate women into the workforce to enable their full participation in economic and social affairs. The Ministry of Labour and Social Affairs took a particularly active role in this regard by setting up a number of committees. These committees have also played an active role in coordinating government's relations with the international women's organisations.

Women in Labour Force

Women account for 35 per cent of the workforce, up from only 5 per cent when independence was achieved in 1971. Women are especially well represented in the public sector making up 57 per cent of employees in education and 53 per cent of medical staff. In the 1970s women were primarily employed in the fields of education and health care. However, in the last twenty years opportunities have opened up for women in fields such as banking and the service industries. This is mainly due to the efforts taken up by the government, thanks to the appointment of women in high profile posts. In 2001 the Emir, Sheikh Hamad bin Isa Al-Khalifa, appointed the country's first female ambassador to the position of envoy to Paris, where she represented Bahrain in its relations with France, Italy, the European Union and Vatican. In the first time in its history in 2002, the government appointed the country's first female deputy minister. It is decided that Women will have the franchise in elections for the session of the Consultative Council beginning in 2004. (Bahrain Brief Issue 6, July 2000).

Political Rights

Always women have been granted the same political rights as men, since the principle of equality between citizens has provided the basis of Sheikh Hamad's reformist agenda. The importance given to women is clear from the fact that there is an information centre for women and children at Isa Town in Bahrain.

Voluntary associations of women

Table 2.2

List of Voluntary Associations of Women as on 1999

Name of Society	*Year of Foundation*
Voluntary Women Societies	
Bahrain Young Ladies Association	1955
Children and Mother Welfare	1960
Awal Women Association	1970
'Riffa Cultural Association	1970
International Women Association	1974

Source: Govt of Bahrain, Website

The power of self-expression enjoyed by the women of the kingdom is revealed from the fact that there are many voluntary organizations of women. Prominent among them are displayed in table 2.2. Apart from this, there are 68 professional, cultural and social societies in Bahrain as on December1999. In addition to this the kingdom has an active independent women's organisation and Bahrain Society for Human Rights for protecting human rights.

On the international arena Bahrain has played a significant role in the promotion of women's rights and equal development. The country has been an active participant at the various United Nations Women's Summits, beginning with the Mexico Conference in 1975. A delegation of Bahraini women represented the country at the landmark Cairo Population and Development Conference of 1994 and at the UN's international women's conference in Beijing in 1995.

Just as in the labour market women have found employment outside the traditional domains of healthcare and teaching, within civil society there has been a gradual move by women's organisations away from a focus on so-called "soft" issues, such as maternity care, to more complex debates, such as women's legal rights within the family.

Discussion of women's political rights was a feature of the recent public debates called by the Amir on the issue of widening the democratic process. Many a times, TV programmes like Hayakom Ma'ana (You Are Welcome With Us), are arranged by devoting a live phone in discussion to the issue of women's political emancipation.

Political equality between men and women is a key component of the recent reforms announced by the Prime Minister Sheikh Khalifa bin Salman al-Khalifa.

Chapter Three

Women Emigrants in the Middle East

Impact of Globalisation on Migration

While the earlier theories on migration concentrated on the push-pull theory, the contemporary views deviate from it. The push - pull theory states that, people migrated either because social and economic forces in the country of origin impelled them to do so, or because they were attracted to places of destination by one or more social and economic factors there. Though the push and pull factors of the international migration generally remain economic (Gulati and Modi, 1983), there is the other dimension of the individuals' decision also. What used to earlier be purely economic reasons for migrating no longer hold in many cases. Globalisation of communication technology has affected extensively the original impetus of individuals to migrate. Linkages between receiving and sending countries are readily established. Networks connect migrants and non-migrants, where news and information are shared. This acts as a catalyst in the flow of migration. Studying networks, particularly those linked with families and households. provides an understanding in the development and encouragement in promoting migration.

While family reunion has been the basic reason for immigration in USA, migration to Middle East is predominantly in search of employment or after securing employment. Studies indicate that in many cases of pre-arranged employment family members play a vital role. Chain migration, especially in family units is of special interest to migration researches. On the aspect of direct labour recruitment, where family reunification is often not possible, increased migration is still evident because of networking. Job opportunities are readily shared. Earlier migrants assist subsequent migrants with accommodations, jobs, and contacts. Inspired by this, new entrants to labour force also undertake further migration.

Impact on Countries of Origin

Migration has tremendous impact on country of origin in improving its economic well-being. Filipinos case can be cited in this regard. They migrate in large numbers in search of a job. The huge remittances to their home country would improve the standard of living considerably. As a result, their status in the community goes up. It is estimated that Filipinos abroad remit approximately $7 B to the Philippine economy. As a result, in the past, Philippinos always remitted huge sum of money to the domestic economy. A large group of NGOs demand that these remittances be used for structural changes to reduce the intensity of migration. Nevertheless, individual or micro-level processes show their impact on the macro-level. Migrant groups abroad were gradually formed. These migrant associations pool their resources and provide funds for projects in home communities. Many organisations here have helped repair local churches in the Philippines, to expand library facilities, or to build playgrounds. Remittances have therefore improved the lives of community members outside migrant families. However, migration has also an impact in the social lives of both the migrants and the families left behind. Statistics show that more than 50 percent of Philippine are migrants.

Migration has various implications. Families may be indefinitely separated, resulting in the alienation of their children. Parents' closeness to their offspring is adversely affected. The husband-wife relationship deteriorates due to long separation. It is not unusual to hear of extra-marital affairs by the husband while the wife is abroad. However, this is not the trend always. Studies indicate that marriage and family life have generally remained stable. Women migrants experience isolation especially when language is totally foreign. They are also forced to live in a foreign culture that has low regard for poorer countries. Abuse in many forms is common in these situations. Increase in consumerism has also been one of the criticisms brought about by remittances sent to families. The creation of global culture brought about by the revolution in mass communications has promoted foreign influences through films, music, TV and videos. Filipinos as trend setters is evident from the large consumption of costly brands of T shirts such as Lacoste and Nike. These remittances have also created a dependency attitude to the recipients. The motivation for self-realization has been overshadowed by expectations upon migrating. In some cases, the remittances to families have become contra-productive.

Impact at Migrant's Destination

Migration has tremendous impact on the receiving country as far as customs, practices and behavioural patterns are concerned. Smaller branches of the original culture are recreated in host countries, such as "Little Italy" or Chinatown, in New York and Los Angeles. Multi-ethnicity is seen in large urban communities. However, a multicultural society may be threatening to native-born citizens of receiving countries. This can elicit resentment among the local population triggering social conflicts. Migration politics in many Western countries are not integrative. The effect of these policies is the marginalisation of migrant workers which results in securing unskilled jobs with low income. It may also bring out unequal opportunities, prejudice and discrimination.

Gender Perspective in Migration

Gender perspective in migration has acquired tremendous importance these days. The presence of women in family promotes family reunion. When women migrate, that responsibility is entrusted on the husband. Current trends, however, show that women are migrating independently. New migratory flows are no longer male-dominated. There is a growing demand for female labour and new social needs have created a demand for services in which only immigrant women are prepared to work which results in the feminisation of migration. There exists a gender-based division of labour in structured activities in a society. Not only do men and women undertake different tasks, but women are responsible for activities in the domestic sphere. These different tasks are the basis for the social construction of gender in which women are excluded from some activities, confined to others, dependent on males, docile, subservient and assigned secondary status in the labour market. They often take up the menial and low-paid occupations, with particularly difficult working conditions. There are women migrants working as domestic servants or as entertainers vulnerable to sexual exploitation. Women migrants are looked down upon due to stereotypes that devalue women and women's work. Migrant women are vulnerable to gender-related violence like rape, sexual harassment and physical abuse. One other serious global problem is trafficking in women. Migration is very much in the core of trafficking in women - in the entertainment industry, domestic workers, child prostitutes - all of which violate fundamental human rights. The important economic contribution by migrant women, particularly the invisible work of the domestic helpers, must be appreciated. Migrant women should enjoy the same privileges and opportunities as other women in the society. The gender-agenda should be top priority in designing migration policies.

Migration can be viewed in terms of restructuring of gender relations. This restructuring need not necessarily be expressed through a satisfactory professional life. It may take place through the assertion of autonomy in social life, through relations with family of origin, or through participating in networks and formal associations. The differential between earnings in the country of origin and the country of immigration may in itself create such autonomy, even if the job in the receiving country is one that does not enjoy higher status in society.

The Middle East and South Asia region is marked by labour migration from less developed to more developed areas, primarily from Pakistan, India, Sri Lanka and Bangladesh to the Gulf oil exporters, where foreigners are 50 to 80 percent of residents. Gulf countries are increasingly concerned about the presence of large number of immigrants. Some countries have adopted restrictive policies aimed at reducing dependence on foreign workers in the private sector and deporting unauthorised foreigners.

In South East Asia, unemployed emigrate for temporary employment to the Middle East. Generally such a move takes place from poorer to richer countries within the region, as from Indonesia to Malaysia. Restrictive policies are adopted in the region and are relaxed under pressure from local employers, as in Thailand and Malaysia, where governments first announce recruitment freezes or reductions in the number of migrants permitted, and them relent when employers complain. Singapore and Malaysia have high percentages of migrants in their work forces, 27 and 12 percent respectively. Sub-Saharan Africa is marked by a wide variety of migrants including refugees to migrants moving over ill-defined orders to the recruitment of high-level professionals. During the 1990s, there were several mass refugee flows, as those from Rwanda. However, uneven economic growth rates have stimulated labour migration flows, as migrants headed for South Africa or the Ivory Coast, where they were sometimes made scapegoats for local economic problems.

On the other hand, the export of domestic workers has become an increasingly important source of earning foreign exchange for the Indian economy. It is a form of labour absorption while chronic unemployment persists in the country. For migrants' families, the remittances are an important supplement for household incomes. The high demand for domestic workers abroad is attributed to the fact that as the educated women in countries experiencing high economic growth enter the labour force, there is an increasing reliance on the import of migrant women to handle domestic work, e.g. household maintenance, and care for the young, the old, and the sick.

Major receiving countries of Indian domestic helpers are the Gulf States, Hong Kong and Singapore. Of these countries, only Hong Kong provides a legal contract so as to protect their rights. For those migrating to other countries, there often is a "contract" that describes the terms of employment. However, this contract is neither binding nor enforced by the laws of the receiving country. Sometimes the conditions of the contract are ignored completely. In the Gulf States, the contract signed in the sending country is often replaced with a new contract which offers considerably less than the original contract. Since there is either very minimal or no protection offered to the legal or documented migrant domestic workers, their working conditions are very pathetic. For those migrating illegally, the situation is worse.

A study about domestic workers was done in 1995. Most of them were between 25 and 40 years of age, majority of them married, but were either separated, divorced, or abandoned. Their husbands had physically and psychologically abused them. The burden of supporting their own children and other family dependents forced them to leave their families and search for work. Recently, trends indicate that younger, unmarried women, commonly between 18-25 years of age, arrive with a dream of working abroad to attain financial security, with little knowledge that they have severe problems to tackle.

Changing Gender Profile of Migrants

Contemporary migration patterns differ considerably from previous migrations. While migration in the past was for permanent resettlement, present-day migration is characterised by temporary overseas employment by leaving the family at the country of origin. A second distinctive characteristic of migration is the role of state in promoting overseas employment. This source of much-needed foreign revenues has become even more important in the present situation. The recent Asian crisis has aggravated unemployment and under-employment all over the globe. The third and most important distinction of contemporary migration is large number of women migrant workers from countries like Philippines, Indonesia, Sri Lanka, Bangladesh and India.

In the whole migration process the mediating agents are the recruitment agencies, which view this as a highly profitable business. Their profitability brightens when desperate women and men from rural areas and urban poor communities attempt to migrate for securing employment.

Female labour migration, particularly of Asians, is characterised by a concentration in gender specific jobs that is menial, low-paying, with poor working conditions and with limited prospects.

These jobs are domestic help, factory work and entertainment. These jobs manifest women's vulnerabilities because the service conditions are not well defined and are not covered or protected by labour laws.

The migration of women workers is demand-driven, usually dictated by the rules and regulations set by the receiving countries. The demand is created by increasing levels of prosperity of developed economies and changing lifestyles in which women nationals leave menial and domestic work for better career opportunities.

The increasing number of women migrant workers in the last 20 years not only reflects the changing patterns in migratory flows but also the increasing and vital role of women in the development of their economies.

Health and Reproductive Rights Issues in Migration

Migrant women who may or may not be trafficked are also exposed to many possible health and reproductive health risks due to the following factors.

First, many of the migrant women workers are below 30 years of age. The Philippines, for instance, sends entertainers or domestic workers as young as 18. The United Arab Emirates admits workers as young as 16 and Malaysia specifies the age of domestic workers to be between 25-45 years of age. Very often, though, traffickers can easily produce fraudulent papers to falsify age requirements so younger and younger women are able to migrate.

In short migration for employment occurs when women are single and are in their prime reproductive years.

Contract substitution is an unwritten practice in many receiving countries where migrant women are paid less salary when compared to the one recorded in their official work contracts. This leads to the women scrimping on their personal needs including medication and health requirements so as to send more money for relatives.

Moreover, it is a regular practice for employers and recruitment agents to shift the place of work of women in violation of their contracts. In this process, women lose control over the terms and conditions and has to totally depend on her employers. The language barrier and ignorance of existing labour laws pose serious problems in negotiating for better working conditions. There are complaints that they are often not given enough food allowance and almost always no medical allowance. They often end up self-medication in cases of illnesses (July-August 1999).

In the Middle East, domestic workers who run away from cruel treatment or attempted rape by their employers are immediately deported regardless of whether they were guilty or not.

Harassment Meted out During Work

A study titled "Punishing the Victim: Rape and Mistreatment of Asian Maids in Kuwait" was conducted by a NGO based at Middle East in 1995. It brought out the fact that domestic workers of Indian, Bangladeshi, Sri Lankan, and Philippine origin were targets of rape, physical assault, non- payment of salaries, debt, bondage and abusive work conditions because of their nationality. Although these abuses are illegal under Kuwaiti law, very few cases are prosecuted as the study pointed out. The New York-based human rights organisation cited the case of the plight of two housemaids to the Emir of Kuwait: a Sri Lankan domestic worker who was raped and thrown from a third floor balcony and a Filipino who jumped from the window of the fourth floor after she was raped by her employer. In a 1996 report on Xenophobia and Racism, the United Nations stated that, immigrants have become easy scapegoats and sacrificial victims of the economic crisis through out the globe. It further added that a large majority of immigrants - mostly from Bangladesh, India, Indonesia, Myanmar, Pakistan, the Philippines and Sri Lanka - consist of women and are subject to double discrimination, that is, both as women and as migrants. The International Labour Organisation (ILO) has discovered numerous cases of maltreatment, sexual harassment and abuses, excessive workload and working for an extra household. Non-completion of contracts and premature returns, especially among women migrating to the Middle East, has been interpreted as indicative of the stressful nature of their situation, according to the report. The Middle East Watch report estimated that for the 12 months beginning in May 1991, 1,400 Filipino domestic servants and hundreds of Indian, Bangladeshi and Sri Lankan maids sought refuge in their home embassies. Salma Khan of the Committee on the Elimination of Discrimination against Women says that the abuses committed against female migrant workers were of great concern to her Committee. Khan also said that migrant workers were not provided with the information and training they needed before proceeding to work abroad. Most migrant workers, who leave their spouses and children, had to face new social problems, including broken homes and single parent families. There should be projects to protect migrant women exposed to abuse and those who attempt to return-migrate.

At present, there are millions of women workers, mostly house maids from the Philippines, Sri Lanka, India and Bangladesh, reportedly working under appalling conditions in East Asia and primarily in Middle Eastern countries. According to the ILO report, about 1.5 million Asian women are working abroad, with a large proportion of them in other Asian countries - the Gulf countries and the fast growing Asian economies of the East. According to the countries of origin, there is an aggregate outflow of 8,00,000 female migrant workers a year. Job-placement agencies, it adds, can be useful in facilitating access to scarce overseas jobs, but they can be costly. Often agencies keep the passports of the women. They charge exorbitant fees and provide loans to be paid from future earnings. While migration provides productive labour and an economic lifeline for millions of Asian women, the dramatic plight of unprotected female migrant workers has become an increasing source of public concern. The report points out that while, from a gender perspective, women should be given equal importance in immigration and emigration policies and access to international labour markets,their status as migrants or non-nationals, and as workers in a gender-segregated labour markets, makes them particularly vulnerable to various forms of discrimination, exploitation and abuse. They therefore require special protection.

Policy Issues

The ILO study by Lin Lean Lim and Nana Oishi says that the policy issues are complicated, not only because they involve questions of equality versus protection, but also because they cover both emigration and immigration policies and employment structures and labour laws of both sending and receiving countries. The inherent socio-cultural attitudes and perceptions concerning the role and status of women in family, society and work place - gender biases are not easily amenable to direct policy intervention. The main exporting countries of migrant women are Indonesia, the Philippines, Sri Lanka and Thailand. The main receiving countries are the Middle East countries, particularly Saudi Arabia and Kuwait. In the 1970s, Asian women accounted for less than 15 percent of the Asian migrant workforce of 1,46,400.By 1987, they comprised some 27 percent of the Asian workers who had left that year to work temporarily abroad. Today, the ILO says, the total number of women emigrants outnumbers that of men. In the Philippines, women account for about 60 percent of migrant workers. In Indonesia, for every male migrant there are two female migrants. In Thailand, women emigrants are estimated to be about 25 percent of the total. The number of emigrant Thai women is growing faster than that of men. In Sri Lanka, an airport survey shows that 84 of migrant workers were females, and of them 94 percent were domestic servants. While the recorded data refers only to legal labour migration, and it does not cover women leaving a country legally for other purposes such as tourism or education but end up in taking up employment. Nor does the data cover those leaving a country illegally to work in other countries. Women from other Asian countries too are migrants, though not in large numbers there could be around 1,00,000 Indian women working in the Middle East. Asian women also migrate to work overseas as nurses, doctors, teachers and secretaries. They go not only to the main labour-importing countries in Asia and the Middle East, but also to the traditional receiving countries in Europe.

Migration policy in most Asian countries is oriented towards diminishing the flows of migrant women workers, but the demand for them in receiving countries is increasing. The dilemma facing policy makers, to restrict or regulate emigration, is complicated because regulation often drives the process underground. The effectiveness of measures by labour-exporting countries is minimal if legislation and labour standards are poor in receiving countries. Once migrants leave their home country the protection their own governments can provide is very limited.

Most receiving countries in Asia and the Middle East do not allow the migrant women workers to come with their families, and so the women have to emigrate by themselves. The residence permit of these workers is linked to their employment, and subject to restrictions. Foreign domestic maids in a number of Asian countries are not permitted to change jobs within two years of taking an employment. Asian female migrant labour supply has been very flexible, relative to men or female migrants from other parts of the world. They respond quickly to changing labour markets overseas. Often they migrate in search of better employment and higher income. The migration is often a family survival strategy in the face of negative effects of the structural adjustment programmes in their home countries. A crucial role played by the Asian women in international labour migration has been the primary reason for sending governments in promoting such flows.

The ILO reports that various studies were undertaken to highlight the plight of female migrants in the female-dominated occupations such as domestic workers, entertainment industry which is considered as an euphemism for prostitution, helpers in restaurants and hotels and other labour-intensive occupations. All such jobs are inferior in nature. Local women shun to take up such jobs because of low remuneration, inferior working conditions and limited job prospects and security. Unfair labour conditions and the vulnerability to abuse of women migrants in domestic service and prostitution are possible in such occupations.

The report notes that the domestic worker often embarks on an overseas stint holding on to a domestic helper contract which is more often than not violated or substituted on arrival with discriminatory and unfair labour conditions. Domestic workers are often paid sub-standard salaries, which are sometimes delayed or withheld. A host of other complaints follows; lack of holidays, inadequate food, unsafe accommodation and lack of proper medical benefits to name a few. There have been innumerable cases of sexual harassment and abuse, excessive workload and income-related exploitation. In addition to all these, the saddening fact is that a major proportion of their earnings are siphoned off to intermediaries. Female workers in domestic service or entertainment services are particularly vulnerable since they go into individualised work situations involving greater isolation and lower level of social support.

Under-employment

The report also highlights the extent of 'underemployment' involved. Among Filipino women inclined to migrate abroad to work as domestic servants, 36 percent were found to be either college graduates or under-graduates. For a better income abroad, they understate their qualifications to get inferior jobs. In the host countries they cannot shift jobs to move to a higher skilled category, but those with higher skills may end up in lower jobs. Nurses for example are being forced into domestic service.

Women in Labour Market

While Asian sending countries have played an active role in promoting labour exports, in the final analysis it is more a demand-driven rather than supply-driven phenomenon. The demand from receiving countries for female migrants - domestic workers, nurses or teachers - is more stable than for construction workers. The female migrants are a more reliable source of foreign exchange remittances for the sending country. Sending countries have now come under increasing pressure to protect their workers abroad. But with more sending countries entering the labour export market, there is competition among them while receiving countries have wider choices and cheaper sources of labour. It is also due to the fact that some labour-exporting countries in Asia insists that the minimum standard wage that the overseas employer must pay could be lower for women than for men. But while Pakistan has been willing to de-regulate the labour market towards this end, India has been averse to doing away with minimum wage requirements. The view that removal of minimum wage limits will make Indian workers more competitive is seen as illusory, and the authorities are against a 'wild export drive' that would cause social problems to workers abroad and families at home.

Many Asian countries have developed restrictions on overseas employment - partly to keep certain skilled workers at home and partly to protect vulnerable workers from abuses and exploitation abroad. But governments in imposing restrictions have had to be careful to ensure that they do not end up motivating women and men to use illegal channels for emigration. Countries in South Asia have tend to be relatively restrictive in sending female workers abroad. Of South Asian countries Sri Lanka has been most lax in regulations on emigration of women. But a policy of restricting female migration has its limited effectiveness. Since bans only increase illegal migration, making the women migrating more vulnerable. Sending countries have been adopting national, bilateral and multilateral efforts to protect their emigrant workers.

Bilaterally, sending countries enter into agreements with receiving countries to protect their migrant workers - through operational agreements which are more difficult since it involves commitment from the receiving country. In addition, the report suggests, both governments have to cooperate to reduce illegal migration, and impose harsh penalties on illegal recruitment agencies and unscrupulous employers. As for multilateral approaches, the study notes that the political sensitivity of the issue has prevented a regional dialogue in Asia. There has also not been solidarity among sending countries for fear of losing their 'market share' to others, especially in the context of the current global downturn. The ILO has established two major conventions and recommendations. One among them is the convention on Migration for Employment(1949), and another is pertaining to Migrant Workers Convention and Recommendations (1975). There are also other conventions of relevance such as the Equality of Treatment(1925), the Social Security(1962), the Maintenance of Social Security Rights (1982) and the one of Social Security for Seafarers (1987). Although the UN adopted an International Convention on Protection of Rights of All Migrant Workers and their Families in 1990, that Convention has not yet come into force. It needs 20 ratifications for entry into force, and as of July 1995 there had only been five ratifications - Egypt, Colombia, Morocco, the Philippines and Seychelles. Mexico and Chile have signed, but not ratified it. But none of the conventions specifically mentioned the plight of female migrant workers. They also have a number of limitations, for example, the supervisory mechanisms function only for those who have ratified a convention. Neither the ILO nor the UN has an enforcement mechanism - beyond collective political pressure. The report suggests recourse to other measures, including educating potential migrants and ensuring availability of information, including encouraging return migrants to talk about their experiences and use of the mass media. Another is fuller and more effective use of NGOs. Sending countries should also seek more active cooperation and networking with NGOs in receiving countries, maintaining strong ties with them through their embassies and consulates. There should also be more concerted international action to protect migrant workers by UN member states. The provision of legal, social and educational opportunities should be provided to migrant women. Chakravarthi Raghavan is the Chief Editor of the South-North Development Monitor (SUNS) from which this article first appeared. It is a fact that in the last two decades more and more Asian women are leaving their families and countries to work abroad especially in the oil-rich Middle East.

Key Issues

Indian migrant workers, including domestic helpers, face various difficulties with their new jobs at the place of migration. Contract-related conflicts are one of the more common problems. In the Middle East in particular, the practice of providing two contracts is rampant. Migrant workers with two contracts are more vulnerable to exploitation. At the work place, the migrant worker may be forced to sign a fresh contract which is usually in Arabic. This contract is often signed by the migrant worker without understanding it. Such contracts are likely to be in favour of the employer.

Moreover, migrant workers rarely receive any copies of their contracts. The contracts signed in India are rendered invalid at the place of migration since the laws are different. Consequently, workers' salaries, nature of work, benefits and period of vacation are reduced to minimum. Sometimes, the provisions are totally removed, making it more difficult for migrants to claim benefits or file a complaint when disputes eventually arise. Some domestic workers are also required by their employers to submit their travel documents to ensure that they do not run away. While employers are required to register their workers, they often wilfully neglect such obligations in order to harass or extort money from their employees when they need to renew their working permits.

Measures to Improve Welfare of Migrant Women in Various Arab Countries

The Asia Pacific regional programme seeks to address the human rights of female migrant workers, both in terms of their working conditions as well as in terms of their legal protection, social and economic status.As a first step to assess the situation of migrant workers in a receiving country, the country suggested the need for a dialogue between government agencies.

In October 2000, a regional UNIFEM meeting was held in Kathmandu of Nepal. It initiated a regional dialogue between governments, experts, NGOs of five selected sending countries such as Nepal, Sri Lanka, Indonesia, the Philippines and receiving countries about women migrant workers regarding ongoing initiatives and good practices.

The overall objective of the project which will be implemented over the period of three years, is to improve the legal, social and economic situation and status of women migrant workers in Jordan through partnerships with the Ministry of Labour in Jordan, the (ILO) and the Sri Lankan Embassy, in addition to a number of other concerned institutions.

The projects were set up to review the Labour Law to cover migrant women workers and to establish coordination between the different stakeholders on both sending and receiving countries. In addition to setting up a database on migrant women workers in Jordan to provide accurate information for stakeholders administering the process, it is aimed at conducting training sessions.

The challenges facing women migrant workers should be met for strong empowerment and rights based approach and its advocacy role. Facilitating cross-country learning is essential to promote joint advocacy support of international conventions and to initiate dialogue between countries of origin and destination.

A research conducted in Bahrain by Munasinghe (2001) about female domestic workers of Sri Lanka, brought out the fact that in 1999,private remittances from the Middle East were 62 percent of total private remittances and 17 percent of national savings.

The following table brings to light the ratio of male and female workers from Srilanka from 1986 to 1999.

Table 3.1

Departures for Foreign Employment by Gender - 1986-1999

Year	*Female (%)*	*Male (%)*
1986	33	67
1987	34	66
1988	55	45
1989	65	35
1990	64	36
1991	67	33
1992	65	35
1993	65	35
1994	73	27
1995	73	27
1996	74	27
1997	75	25
1998	66	34
1999	65	35

Source: Sri Lanka Bureau of Foreign Employment

Contact CENWOR for additional information

A large number of women are moving into labour force in Asia, but they occupy bottom rungs of the employment ladder leading to increase in the scale and risk of sexual harassment at workplaces, says a technical report of I LO. The report says that women now comprise an increasing share of world's labour force, at least one-third in several regions of the world.

In most of the Asian countries, the share is even higher. The percentage of women registered as part of the labour force in 1995-97 amounts to well over 40 per cent in East, South-East and Central Asia, and approximately one-third in South Asia.

At the same time, the report says, the majority of Asia's women workers are observed to be in jobs with low security, low pay, inferior conditions of work, low status and having low bargaining power with more probability of being subjected to sexual harassment.

Similarly, foreign workers in domestic service, the isolation may be even more pronounced. They lack support from local community, and may be more afraid of reporting harassment. Their numbers are increasing.

The process of emigration of skilled and educated labour from India to the Middle East Countries is a well known fact and is a fascinating subject of study from the economic, sociological and psychological points of view. Though the push and pull factors of the international migration generally remain economic (Gulati and Modi, 1983), there are other dimension of the individuals' decision also.The present study throws some light on the Indian Migrant women in the labour market of Bahrain.

A study is undertaken by personally visiting the Middle East Country particularly Bahrain so as to ensure that the information is authentic and dependable. Since large number of women migrate to find better avenues for utilising their education or professional skills, it was felt necessary to interact with women emigrants at their emigration country.

The researcher has attempted to interact with recently arrived female emigrants from India on the basis of information received from their friends. The purpose is to collect latest information about Indian migrant in leading professions in Bahrain.

Chapter Four

Emigrant Women in Leading Professions

The Teaching Profession

The interaction with the employed women migrants during my stay in Bahrain aimed at obtaining a comprehensive analysis of professions in which they predominate. It transpired that the golden era of migration is over due to the trend of localisation and provision of better education which have gathered momentum in the Kingdom. A comparative analysis of women are in various professions in Bahrain was done to gather information about emigrants in labour market. By making a list of the opportunities available for the migrants, it was found that majority of them are into only a few professions such as teaching, nursing, stenography, office secretaries' posts and domestic maids. It is widely considered that some form of teaching is the obvious opening for educated women, who aspire to achieve economic independence. But thanks to the various causes and developments, it is now almost universally recognised that teaching is a profession in which one can enter only by proper training. Under each profession the writer has given an attempt to describe the nature of work, special training required,rate of remuneration and suggestions for improvement in conditions of work, on the basis of available information.

The Type of Management

Most of the schools in Middle East are operated by private management. The only exception is the Indian Embassy School,which is managed by the respective elected body chaired by Indian Ambassador.

Indian teachers are mostly working in Indian curriculum schools. There are other schools which follow British curriculum, where Indian teachers are very rare. The salary structure for British curriculum schools are much better compared to that of the Indian curriculum schools. Lack of external financial assistance compels the private schools to operate as a business house rather than a service oriented institution. The private management is operating to make profit in this business. Some teachers complained that private management has developed a trend of not appointing talented teachers as they have to pay handsome salary and perks. Though there are exceptional cases, most of the private schools function with profit motive and therefore they select housewives of expatriates as teachers by paying comparatively lower salary. However, there are few female teachers who excel in their field by training and teaching experience.

Mode of Recruitment

Approximately 90 percent of the teachers in the school are females. The reason for such a large number of females taking up teaching profession is that most of them are housewives,who accompany their husbands in the process of migration. During post-migration phase they take up the job as a school teachers. The private managements find it easy to recruit teachers from locally migrated candidates, since they can earn lucrative profits by way of not paying good salary, housing, and air ticket. Further, private schools often terminate teachers' services without providing any service benefits or prior notice.

Since teachers are being recruited in this manner in private schools, the credibility of teaching standard is definitely in question. Most of the teachers are not trained properly and this adversely affects the performance of students.

The Salary Structure

The salary structure for the teachers in private schools is very poor. It varies from US $ 320 to US $ 400. But in Indian Embassy Schools, better salary is provided ranging from US $ 650 to US $ 800.(for international comparison purpose salaries are expressed in terms of US Dollar, where as the value of Dollar in terms of Bahrain Dinar is 0.377).

Teachers do not enjoy any other benefits like free housing, yearly paid vacation, transportation allowances and yearly air tickets to home country.

Teachers can earn extra money by way of private tuitions, ranging from US $ 55 to US $ 65 per student per month. There are many female teachers who earn handsome amount of money from tuitions. Most of the teachers engage private tuitions at their house, and make additional income in the range of US$ 300 to US$ 700 per month. So by dint of hard work, they try to make up for the poor salary.

It should be noted that in good private schools where the teaching standards are equally high, the salaries are approximately on the same level as in embassy schools.

But private schools are enormously in standing, when they are inferior; the teachers are not paid adequate salary.

Private schools are usually held in good standing. But if the standard is poor, the teachers are not paid adequate salary.

The best private schools, on the other hand, meet a real need and, as a large proportion of their pupils do not enter for public examination, it is possible for them, to make valuable experiments which could not easily be tried in larger subsidised institutions.

Nature of Contract

Unfortunately in Bahrain teachers do not get any proper contract agreement from their employers. On the basis of unwritten bilateral agreement, terms and conditions pertaining to their employment is finalized

Working Time

Other than Indian Embassy schools all other private schools are on single shift. The double shift is from 6.30a.m to 12.30p.m and 1p.m to 6p.m while the single shift is from 6.30a.m to 1 p.m. In short, the total working constitute 6 hours per day and 6 days a week.

Fees

The private schools have to raise the funds by collecting fees from students as the government does not provide any grants or monetary support to any school. Private schools are usually held in good standing. But if the standard is poor, the teachers are not paid adequate salary.The school charges a fee of approximately US $ 55 per student, up to seventh standard. The fees charged varies in the range of US $ 65 -75 for higher classes up to twelfth standard. Most of the Middle East countries do not have a university which gives admission to expatriate students. Bahrain attained such unique status by 2002 as it has permitted expatriate students to continue their higher education in the Kingdom.

Nature of Work

As a class, teachers are badly paid and many are overworked. The physical and mental strain is invariably severe, in many cases this is unnecessarily increased by red-tape regulations that involve loss of time and temper. The amount of clerical work which teachers have to complete serves no useful purpose. It does enrich their teaching talents or experience.

Details of Students and Teachers for Various Courses

Apparently the policy, as evidenced in most of Arab countries is to discourage women students from undertaking higher education, Bahrain encourages girl students to acquire education.

Students who desire to do advanced work will need at least one, and probably two, additional years at the University, while all women who intend to teach in schools ought to spend one year in training. Schools of all types mentioned and a few others, providing education at least from ten to sixteen, years of age, are known as secondary schools.

Table 4.1 provides more details pertaining to the male and female students registered for various branches of discipline at secondary level in Bahrain. Previously higher education was restricted to only locals after attaining 18 years. As a part of reforms introduced in 2002, now non-Bahraini students also can continue education even after completing 18 years of age. The number of non-Bahraini children opted for certain courses are very less as reflected in table 4.1. For example those opted for animal husbandry as well as printing are practically nil.

Table 4.2 provides details of government education with special reference to number of schools, classes, teachers and students from 1974 –75 to 1998-99.The table does not contain information of administrative and technical staff required in the field of education. Till 1982-83, male teachers were more than females, though the trend changed later.

Table 4.1

Secondary School Students by Nationality and Gender (96/1997 - 98/1999)

	Nationality / Gender								
	Total			*Non - Bahraini*			*Bahraini*		
	Total	*Females*	*Males*	*Total*	*Females*	*Males*	*Total*	*Females*	*Males*
					96/1997				
Science	6,983	4,257	2,726	583	261	322	6,400	3,996	2,404
Literary	7,908	5,215	2,693	214	138	76	7,694	5,077	2,617
Agriculture and Animal Husbandry	3	0	3	0	0	0	3	0	3
Catering	81	0	81	4	0	4	77	0	77
Textiles	92	92	0	1	1	0	91	91	0
Printing	44	0	44	0	0	0	44	0	44
Advertising	87	87	0	3	3	0	84	84	0
Religious Education	59	0	59	25	0	25	34	0	34
Industrial	3,192	0	3,192	64	0	64	3,128	0	3,128
Commercial	3,788	2,091	1,697	132	70	62	3,656	2,021	1,635
Total	**22,237**	**11,742**	**10,495**	**1,026**	**473**	**553**	**21,211**	**11,269**	**9,942**

(Table Contd...)

(Table Contd...)

	Nationality / Gender								
	Total			*Non - Bahraini*			*Bahraini*		
	Total	*Females*	*Males*	*Total*	*Females*	*Males*	*Total*	*Females*	*Males*
					97/1998				
Science	7,291	4,522	2,769	544	259	285	6,747	4,263	2,484
Literary	6,944	4,569	2,375	198	115	83	6,746	4,454	2,292
Catering	16	0	16	0	0	0	16	0	16
Textiles	108	108	0	1	1	0	107	107	0
Printing	22	0	22	0	0	0	22	0	22
Advertising	96	96	0	0	0	0	96	96	0
Religious Education	59	0	59	20	0	20	39	0	39
Industrial	3,136	0	3,136	45	0	45	3,091	0	3,091
Commercial	4,425	2,344	2,081	126	64	62	4,299	2,280	2,019
Total	**22,097**	**11,639**	**10,458**	**939**	**439**	**495**	**21,163**	**11,200**	**9,963**

(Table Contd...)

(Table Contd...)

	Nationality / Gender								
	Total			*Non - Bahraini*			*Bahraini*		
	Total	*Females*	*Males*	*Total*	*Females*	*Males*	*Total*	*Females*	*Males*
					98/1999				
Science	7,592	4,805	2,787	549	281	268	15,888	4,524	2,519
Literary	6,078	3,982	2,096	210	116	94	5,868	3,866	2,002
Catering	9	0	9	0	0	0	9	0	9
Textiles	128	128	0	0	0	0	128	128	0
Advertising	130	130	0	0	0	0	130	130	0
Religious Education	56	0	56	9	0	9	47	0	47
Industrial	3,294	0	3,294	81	0	81	3,213	0	3,213
Commercial	5,173	2,839	2,334	148	80	68	45,778	2,759	2,266
Total	**22,460**	**11,884**	**10,576**	**997**	**477**	**520**	**21,463**	**11,407**	**10,056**

Source: Govt of Bahrain, Website

Table 4.2

Government Education (No. of Students, Teachers, Classes and Schools) (1974/75-1998/99)

Academic Year	*Total No. of Schools*		*Total No. of Classes*			*Distribution of Teachers*			*Distribution of Students*	
	Females	*Males*	*Females*	*Males*	*Total*	*Females*	*Males*	*Total*	*Females*	*Males*
1974/75	51	64	704	886	2,696	1,194	1,502	57,740	25,854	31,886
1975/76	51	62	725	894	2,870	1,308	1,562	59,497	26,713	32,784
1976/77	50	62	731	889	2,786	1,303	1,483	60,872	27,332	33,540
1977/78	49	65	755	976	3,079	1,439	1,640	62,621	28,321	34,300
1978/79	50	69	798	1,006	3,386	1,618	1,768	65,162	29,424	35,738
1979/80	54	68	864	1,045	3,557	1,735	1,822	67,379	30,502	36,877
1980/81	57	68	902	1,071	3,761	1,844	1,917	69,083	31,625	37,458
1981/82	57	68	924	1,093	3,990	1,961	2,029	71,177	32,951	38,226
1982/83	57	69	995	1,162	4,409	2,158	2,251	75,434	35,460	39,974
1983/84	60	71	1,073	1,223	4,740	2,377	2,363	78,797	37,320	41,477
1984/85	61	73	1,135	1,269	4,803	2,427	2,376	82,699	39,947	42,752
1985/86	63	76	1,199	1,326	4,931	2,513	2,418	85,867	41,880	43,987

(Table Contd...)

(Table Contd...)

Academic Year	*Total No. of Schools*		*Total No. of Classes*			*Distribution of Teachers*			*Distribution of Students*	
	Females	*Males*	*Females*	*Males*	*Total*	*Females*	*Males*	*Total*	*Females*	*Males*
1986/87	66	77	1,261	1,366	4,967	2,615	2,352	88,132	43,244	44,888
1987/88	69	78	1,297	1,398	5,157	2,729	2,428	90,734	44,549	46,185
1988/89	71	80	1,352	1,433	5,368	2,599	2,769	92,862	45,835	47,027
1989/90	74	81	1,402	1,488	5,670	2,746	2,924	95,724	47,339	48,385
1990/91	76	82	1,498	1,554	5,834	2,859	2,975	100,658	50,055	50,603
1991/92	80	82	1,570	1,645	5,978	3,291	2,687	101,070	50,397	50,673
1992/93	80	82	1,682	1,684	6,444	3,599	2,845	104,205	51,954	52,251
1993/94	83	84	1,666	2,492	6,552	3,774	2,778	106,599	53,273	53,326
1994/95	86	88	1,740	2,376	6,661	3,889	2,772	108,606	54,287	54,319
1995/96	90	90	1,783	1,878	6,825	4,075	2,750	109,890	55,089	54,801
1996/97	90	92	1,816	1,882	6,676	4,070	2,606	110,161	55,527	54,634
1997/98	94	94	1,862	1,907	6,936	4,210	2,726	111,443	56,339	55,104
1998/99	94	96	1,881	1,897	6,771	4,139	2,632	113,043	57,278	55,765

1. Excluding Administrative and Technical Staff

Source: Govt of Bahrain, Website

This could be due to the fact that more women started to acquire higher education and started to participate actively in the labour market after 1982-83. Thus the number of female teachers exceeded over males with effect from 1983-84.

Nature of Training

It is still desirable to emphasise on the fact that the untrained women teacher finds it increasingly difficult to obtain a satisfactory teaching post. Modern language or English specialists will need practical training in phonetics, for example, mathematics teachers require to study modern methods of teaching their subjects. The best training colleges ofcourse provide for such training. University training department have the advantage over others, since they can secure the services of experts for the discussion of their subjects.

There remains lastly the case of student who, while definitely desiring to teach wishes at the same time to go on with her own work, to undertake for research or advanced or independent studies. Such a one will aim for University or college appointment in the hope of pursuing her own work under congenial conditions.

During the training period the intending teacher must, if this is not already determined, decide on the special branch for which she wishes to prepare, according to her qualifications and the needs of schools. If actual teaching experience can first be obtained for two or three years, it enables earning to begin at once and greatly increases the value of training taken subsequently.

Sex-prejudice

At almost all the new universities men and women are nominally equally eligible for every teaching post. In practice women are rarely selected for the higher positions.

Sex prejudice is often pointed out as the reason for this discrimination. It may be assumed that between two candidates of equal qualifications, preference will definitely be given to the man. The simple reason for large number of women to take up school teaching profession in the Kingdom is that men are not interested in it due to poor remuneration. It is certain that the woman should have higher qualification and should be more distinguished than her male competitors to stand her chance of professional appointment. It is also true in the case of co-educational universities also.

Pensions

Contributory pension schemes for the professorial body for permanent assistances in receipt of a special income has been compulsorily established in the case of all non-migrants as explained in Chapter 1. But in Middle East countries and in Bahrain the scheme of providing pension to expatriate workers does not exist. It has been known that Saudi Arabian Oil Company (ARAMCO) Saudi Arabia pays it to workers.

Maternity-leave

The maternity leave is not sanctioned for expectant mothers. However, 75 days leave can be accumulated by working on off-days by planning in advance. The severe criticism leveled against Middle East Countries is their lack of empathy towards expectant mothers. It is reported that the country deliberately adopts this policy to discourage migration of the married

However Indian Embassy School stands as an ideal in this regard. Three months maternity leave with half pay is granted to teachers by Embassy School. In other schools leave varying between one to two months is provided without pay.

Teaching in Colleges and Universities

It is certain that the number of university appointments open to local women is on the increase, and that there is no present likelihood that the demand for qualified women will remain stationary. On the other hand, the necessary qualifications, personal as well as intellectual, are high; the work is hard, though attractive and it is in every respect that those whose talents can better be exerted in other branches of the profession should endeavour to obtain college posts. Broadly speaking such opening is of four kinds: -

1. Administrative posts – These are usually the reward of long and successful service in junior appointments.
2. Professorial posts and staff lecturership: these are almost certainly confined to women's colleges though there are some exceptions to this rule.
3. Lecturerships, assistant lecturership and demonstratorships: These are usually open to women in practice as well as in theory though much depends upon the personal idiosyncrasy of the head of the department, and on the importance of the posts and salary offered.
4. Closely allied with University work is the work of training teachers. In training colleges and in university training departments there is a constant demand for lecturers.

Competent girls who can bide their time can usually get a footing in some universities. Their future advancement will depend on value to the institute on original writing and research even more than on their teaching work, on committees and influence with the students. Largely, it will depend on her tact and popularity with her colleagues: to a very considerable extent it still rests also on conditions over which she has no control, and which are part and parcel of the slow recognition of a woman's right to compete on equal terms with men.

It seems as far as can be judged that future opportunities are likely to occur when the right candidates for posts are there in sufficient numbers to make their exclusion on the ground of sex, already seldom explicitly stated, impossible or expedient. Meanwhile, it is probable that, individual women will continue in some cases to unquestionable attainments and strength of personality, they may attain the positions they desire. Slow progress is not altogether bad for the ultimate cause of women at the Universities; nothing could injure that cause so much as mistakes at the initial stage. An important appointment given to the wrong woman, or to one in many respect inferior to her colleagues would not serve any purpose. Bringing right woman to the right post is essential.

University women teachers can be securers of equality of opportunity in many respects. Apart from pursuing their own interest of the present, they must remember that they have to contribute tremendously to learning as well as for teaching. Secondly the equality of payment and status should be insisted and there should not be any discrimination on the basis of gender. Lastly women on committees and elsewhere are not justified in remaining unduly in the background. When they have something worth contributing to the discussion, it is not modesty but lack of business capacity, which makes them silent. Women, who are unwilling or unable to assert themselves when necessary, are not in place at Co-education University. Most women however, will derive intellectual stimulus from the free interchange of opinion, possible only when both sexes are working happily together, with common interests and common aim.

In Women's Colleges there is, of course, no sex bar, and the way lies from the bottom to the top of the ladder. Conditions of appointment, tenure, and work do not greatly differ from those described except in so far as the stipends tend to be lower especially for more responsible posts, when these are ordinarily occupied by women. The most suitable candidate for a post is the one who should be selected, irrespective of sex. It is this principle that women are endeavoring to establish. They must do so by scrupulous fairness when the power is theirs; by making themselves indisputably most fitted, when they are knocking at the closed door.

One further topic needs discussion in this section – the continued employments of married women in University posts. At present there is no universal rule and every case has to be judged on its merits. Every lecturer who marries, can and ought to help from the precedent that the continuance of professional work is a matter for her own decision and is not one that concerns the governing bodies. Already a large number of women, mothers as well as wives, have set good examples and have established their own position, sometimes without question, sometimes as the result of a difficult struggle. It is clear that Universities, with their long vacations, and with their established recognition of long absence for special purposes, have less ground than most employers to raise difficulties for married women.

Problems Faced by Teachers

The salaries paid to the teachers are insufficient to cover charges for maintenance, clothes, books, etc. While considering the expenses incurred during each year of the study at college in the form of fees, for boarding and lodging expenses during vacation, it is required to provide reasonable salary to them. Men candidates are in this respect far more worse off than the female candidates. Married female candidates have yet another source of income to depend upon.

Salaries are bound to remain low, while women are forced to consider their profession as a means to pass time after marriage, and not as a life-work. Managements by knowing this psychology of teachers exploits this situation. Moreover, there are real dangers in entrusting students' education in the hands of under-paid teachers. Further the salaries of assistant teachers vary considerably. In no single instance is a woman teacher paid the same. This is true even if the work is identical in character, as in the case of mixed schools and teacher's centers, salaries of assistant teachers are still less. One of the implication of this inequality of payment is that woman teachers are often employed to teach the lower classes. Some schools are staffed entirely by women, not because women teachers are deemed more suitable for the work, but because her labour is cheaper; hence the need in the teaching profession, for recognition of the principle of "equal pay for equal work." Without it the status of the women becomes lower than that of the man. As a result inferior unqualified women are appointed and it brings in humiliation for the profession. Only when there is equality of pay can there be security that the best candidate will be appointed irrespective of the gender.

Inspite of the building regulations of the Board of Education, some school premises are far from satisfactory with regard to lighting, ventilation, construction and often even cleanliness, these defects naturally have their effects on the health of the teachers.

Another notable difference between India and Bahrain is that teachers are not well prepared or organised for the purpose of self protection.

The localisation policy has gathered momentum in almost all fields in the Kingdom. At the present time there is a strong probability of a dearth of qualified local teachers for elementary schools in the near future. There are several factors which have been influential in bringing about this state of affairs. One is, the uncertainty of employment. Even after a long and comparatively costly training, this defect will be remedied only when a rational method of regulating the supply of teachers is established so that each candidate may be certain, that, if she qualifies, she will be guaranteed employment.

As compared with the assistant mistresses in a secondary school her lot is not altogether enviable. If she has shorter holidays, larger classes, and a lower stipend, these facts must be counterbalanced by remembering that she has comparatively few corrections, much less home work, and no pressure for external examining bodies, that her tenure is far less insecure, and that her training and education have been to a very large extent borne by the State or by local authorities.

The teachers complained about the strain of supervision duties in addition to their work in school, though the salary is poor. When a girl is about to leave school at the age of seventeen or eighteen, she is often as little able to determine what profession she wishes to adopt, as is her brother in the same case. If she is intelligent, well trained and eager to study, her natural impulse is to go to college, and to get there, it is still usually the line of least resistance to say that she wishes to become a teacher. When there are peculiar difficulties in the way, the decision must be taken in still earlier.

Moreover, granted that the desire to teach is a real one, and that the girl has an aptitude, it ought still to be necessary to choose a particular branch of profession before she becomes an under graduate. A university career means among other things, the discovery of new powers, new interests and new opportunities; sometimes it brings with it the painful conviction that aspiration has outstripped its capacity. The bright girl who has excelled at school may find that she is unfit for the work. She is not necessarily worse on that account, but she must substitute some other plan for her ambition to become a specialist. In many cases until the first degree is taken, there is sufficient time to determine the profession, which has to be adopted.

The average pass graduate will do her best to fit herself as an all round form mistress, there should be no reason to determine in what type of school, elementary or secondary. The training required should be the same if the classes, were as ought to be, of manageable size, and the equipment in both types of institution is equally good. Teachers in both kinds of school would benefit the present absurd division between them ceases to exist. Children under fourteen requires similar discipline to whatever their social status, even if the subjects taught are to differ – somewhat a matter which is controversial and need not be discussed here – the teachers need similar training and the same kind and amount of academic education.

Many desirable persons are debarred from entering the teaching profession, because of low remuneration, considering the responsibility of the work; and this drawback is still further emphasised by the very inadequate pension which is offered at the close of the teachers career, this difficulty can be overcome only when the main burden of the cost of education is removed from the private management and placed on the national exchequer.

Suggestions for Improvement

Various as may be their origins and different their aims, the teachers in them form a fairly homogenous group with definite points in common. Teachers need to concentrate their energies on essentials: of these the intellectual life is the most important, and however elementary the standard of work demanded in class. No one can teach freshly unless at the same time, learning and widening her own mental horizon. Additional works like, too many forms to fill up, too many complicated registers to keep, too many meetings to attend, adversely affect the creativity and crush the spirit.

There is not a necessary accompaniment of the profession. Anything, which tends to make teachers' lives narrower, is opposed to the cause of education. This truth should be instilled into all official bosoms.

There will be, of course, much to sadden her in such experiences, but at least they will add a sense of reality to her teaching which will keep her in close touch with life. She will find that there are compensations for hard work and red-tape regulations, even for low remuneration and slowness of promotion. Resulting from the requirements of the board of education, grant is a must. It is paid to most of the schools in other countries.

On the other hand, under existing pressure to relieve the burden of childhood, women must see to it that the mothers of the coming generation are not sacrificed at the earliest stages of the lives of the children that are to be, the motherhood of women and their home – making powers are indeed to be developed, but not at the expense of their own lives and their citizenship. Women educators then must take what is good in boy's education, what has been good in girls and must utilise both. This work is great and it is specially difficult because legislation and administration are almost entirely different and are to be brought up on different lines. Women who see the truth there is in both of these propositions are hindered alike by men who hold the one and those who hold the other.

A woman, whose best work is that of an assistant, should not be tempted to give it up for the salary of a headmistress. The assistant has opportunity for closer and more personal touch with her girls being intimately responsible for a smaller number also, has better opportunities for working out the teaching of her subjects and improving its technique. Education would gain if more of the ablest teachers, specially successful in one or the other of those directions, were left in a position to continue this work, instead of feeling obliged to substitute for it the perhaps uncongenial task of organisers, inspectors, committees and the public which occupies the time of the head schools in this country.

Pensions are not generally provided for any category of teachers in the country. Even in government service it is not provided, though it was provided earlier. Under present conditions, the principle of general equality of income, not yet being considered as a serious proposition, it is surely economically right for the teaching profession to claim remuneration sufficient to give it a status corresponding to the worth and dignity of its work. Above all, women are not entirely dependent on their earnings and therefore, in a position to resist- under-payment should not act as blacklegs and keep down the rate for others dependent for a livelihood on their occupation.

Under-payment for teachers means a narrower, more anxious life than should be theirs who are to live in the strongly electric atmosphere of a body of girls and young women – and yet keep a calm serenity of spirit – a life less full than is essential for those who have to give at all time freely of their best.

Similarly, in order that the fullest possible life may be open to the women teacher, it seems desirable that continuance in the profession after marriage should me more usual than it is.

Some may argue that the married women is in certain ways better suited for young people than her unmarried colleague. Often the most valuable years of a woman's life are lost to the school by her enforced retirement due to marriage. She gives to it her younger less experienced years, when she knows less of the world, less of the problems of the household, less of the outlook of the parents. It must be remembered that the parent's point of view must be important if there is to be coordination between home and school. To the teacher – mother there will come altogether new power of understanding, which should ultimately compensate the school for broken time during the earlier years of the life of her children.

Many secondary teachers will welcome the idea that they need not abandon either the career they have chosen or the prospect or the fullest developments as women. The teaching profession would thus retain many valuable members lost to it on marriage and the ranks of married women recruited by many well suited to be the mothers of citizens.

The career of teaching adolescent girls gives many experiences which others seek for in leisure hours. The woman among other girls had the privilege of handing on to them the keys to the intellectual treasuries where she has enriched herself, of setting their feet in the paths, which have led to her to fruitful fields. She may watch over the birth and growth of the reasoning powers of her pupils and guide them into the great fellowship of workers for truth. It is interesting but not easy work.

Progressive women today resent the social system, which requires them to be economically dependent upon others. They realize that social service needs labour of a highly skilled variety, and they therefore demand, on the one hand, training for their work as a guarantee of their efficiency in its performance, and, on the other hand, monetary payment and security of tenures as guarantees to them. Women's lack of political power, there are no spheres of professional work in which revealing conditions are in these respects completely satisfactory.

To-day parents attitude towards the teacher is normally one of friendly co-operation and respect, with the result that the latter is fast becoming a powerful factor in shaping and influencing the democracy. The school is extending its influence in every sphere, which touches on the social, physical, intellectual and spiritual well being of the people. Activities, which until recently were associated only with institutions, distinctly religious in character and now regularly connected with the work of primary schools. Thus the teacher has every opportunity for the exercise of public spirit, within schools and without. She is daily confronted with the problem of evolving and developing an educated democracy, which will demand and obtain proper conditions of life.

The nature of work asked of the teachers in primary schools, has led to insistence by the state on the necessity for the professional training, as well as for their academic proficiency. These requirements have met with the counter-demand on the part of the teachers. When majority of schools are owned by private management and they raise their money by collecting fees from students, burden of education does not fall on government though it is free and compulsory in the kingdom of Bahrain.

Another factor that tends to make the teaching profession unattractive is the very tenuous life, which it entails under the modern conditions. Again, so far as women are concerned there is not complete security of tenure, though apart from the regulation that obtains under some local authorities, requiring women to resign on marriage, teachers in elementary schools, owing to the efforts of their various organization, posses far greater security of tenure that teachers in any other branch of the profession. Another point in favour of the teachers in elementary schools is their freedom from the burden of extraneous duties and from the nightmare of the external examinations.

When schools can be more generously staffed so that, for example the number of assistant teachers exceeds the number of classes to be taught a good deal will have been done to relieve the strain under which teachers are at present working.

No girl should become a teacher because she does not know how else to gain her living. The profession is lamentably overstocked with mediocrities, lacking enthusiasm and vigour, drifting more and more hopelessly from one post to another. But there is plenty of room for keen and competent women, eager to learn and to teach and this is true of all branches of the profession. No work can well be more thankless, more full of drudgery and of disappointment than that of a teacher who has missed her vocation.

MEDICINE AND NURSING

Medicine

Personal contact with women migrants brought out the fact that there were very few women doctors from India whereas a larger number of men migrant doctors are there. There is a common belief that doctors with U.K or American degree are more efficient while nobody prefer to consult Egyptian Doctors. Post graduate doctors in various fields such as pediatrics, surgery, ENT, dentistry, general practitioners and MBBS degree holders as well as dentists with BDS degree come under the category of migrant doctors. It was also known that few doctors draw very large amount of salary though they did not reveal the actual figures. It has been reliably learnt that a doctor with plain MBBS degree could fetch in a minimum of $800 per month. Reputed hospitals like American Mission Hospitals have appointed many eminent doctors from India, the major chunk of whom belongs to males, as the sources revealed.

The Salary Structure

The remuneration in nursing profession varies according to the type of job, hospital and nature of work. According to 1993 estimates, Bahrain has one doctor per 352 patients and the number of physicians are 1,115. The number of Indian women doctors are very limited in Bahrain though there are large number of female nurses. There is only one medical college, Salmaniya Medical Complex, a 1000 bed teaching hospital attached to Gulf University, which provides degrees and diplomas of medical and para- medical courses.

In any event no woman needs to retire from her work on marriage, though it is, of course, most important that the married medical woman should not deny to herself and to her husband the normal healthy joy of having children.

Details of Hospitals in Bahrain

The government medical college in Bahrain is Salmania Medical Complex Hospital. This is a very big hospital with almost all specialized departments. Various medical and para-medical courses are taught here.

There are big private hospitals in Bahrain like American Mission Hospital. International Hospital and Ibn Al- Nafees Medical Complex in which large number of Indian nurses are working. Egyptian, Srilankan and even Philippine nurses are working there, though less in number. The hospitals in the health sector can be mainly categorised as:

Government hospitals—mostly which are medical colleges with number of beds ranging from 1000 and above.

Hospitals—large private hospitals, number of beds ranging from 50 to 500.

Hospitals—small hospitals number of beds ranging from to 50 to 75.

Clinics—mostly out patient division (OPD).

The hospitals follow some rules and norms set by Health Ministry. Even though government has not fixed minimum wages for nurses working in private hospital. Only government hospital has decided upon a wage scale. Due to this reason the candidates from third world countries like India are exploited by private hospitals. Large number of Bangladeshi, Srilankan and Philippines nurses also working in the Kingdom. However it transpired that most of the private hospitals have kept minimum monthly salary which comes around US $ 240.

Nursing Profession

Interaction with active participants in the labour market of Bahrain brought out the fact that majority of women emigrants from India are nurses. There are virtually no hospitals in Bahrain without any Indian nurse. Their dedicated and service oriented approach invited appreciation from the citizens of several countries.

It may be safely claimed that, although there is still much to be done, in nursing, Indian woman have gained as good a position as in any other branches of labour.

One of the most important considerations in discussing any branch of women's work is what sort of women is suited for it.

Eligibilty for Nursing Candidates

The following are the chief pre-requisites for the nursing profession:

(i) Enthusiasm

The first and most important qualification is enthusiasm. It is impossible to follow nurse's profession with success, unless it is work for which one had natural taste. It necessitates a very strenuous life, and has many unpleasant details of work, which are unimportant to a person to whom the occupation is acceptable as a whole, but which would be quite inseparably disagreeable to any one to whom the total idea of life embodied in it was unattractive.

(ii) Knowledge of human-beings

Another very important qualification is knowledge of people. A nurse must never forget that she is dealing with human nature.

(iii) Good health

A sick nurse is an anomaly and many people prefer to be indifferently nursed by some one who is cheerful and healthy, rather than have the most dedicated service from a woeful person.

(iv) Education

A good general education is essential. This should include a certain amount of intelligence, which is needed throughout the work. The person must also possess the necessary capacity for acquiring knowledge. It is however necessary to posses average intelligence and a good memory and it is difficult for people to pass the qualifying examinations if they have given up school work which is characteristic of the habit of learning large number of new facts.

(v) Adequate Money

Money is a necessary requirement for the successful completion of the course. Money is needed for the three reasons:

(a) The training is more expensive

(b) It is also strenuous, making a certain amount of margin for suitable recreation very desirable

(c) Earning capacity is high when compared to the money spent for education.

So often women enter the labour market only when driven by stark necessity that it is unfortunately the easiest thing in the world to exploit them. People of either sex faced by starvation for themselves or those dependent on them must take the first thing that offers if the conditions were it in any way bearable.

Type of Recruitment

Nurses generally migrate followed by a recruitment in India. Therefore they have a contract agreement with the employer. They get almost all benefits like housing, transportation from house to work and return, yearly paid vacation. They also get yearly or two yearly free air ticket to home country.

Regarding Nursing Qualifications

Before beginning her training the student has to decide what qualification she will take, her choice lies between

(i) A degree of one of the universities and

(ii) A diploma

It is essential to go to some University or Examining Board, which admits women, where women are denied the degree to which their work entitles them. As a matter of fact, women medical students are not accepted at any cost and preference is given to man. It is not possible to practice medicine, in a satisfactory way unless one is actually in possession of the qualification.

In the majority of well-managed hospitals there is an examination to test a nurse's knowledge before she is awarded a certificate. In other hospitals it is merely a question of so many months or years of service, without any test of ability or special fitness. This lack of minimum standard constitutes, at the present time, a danger to the public, and a great injustice to the nursing profession itself. The public has no guarantee that a nurse has learned the special work, which she is engaged to perform, and a trained nurse must compete with unqualified persons who use her title and adopt her dress and often bring her profession into great disrepute.

The almost universally accepted term for general training is three years though the engagement is frequently for four years. The fourth year gives the nurse very valuable experience and is of value to the hospital as it thereby retains, for a certain time, the services of the pupils when they are of the greatest use.

Many women spend five or six years in learning before they finally take posts as private nurses or as Sisters of Hospitals wards, or enter some other branch of profession. A nurse is therefore, seldom less than twenty-five or twenty-six years of age when she begins to practice her profession, and is often still older. The comparatively late age at which the training is started is a drawback, as most begin to train as soon as they leave school at seventeen or eighteen, and have thus found other employment.

The woman who aspires to be a nurse should be well educated, and physically and mentally robust. She must be prepared to give all her energies to the exacting and laborious work, which she will be expected to perform. Intelligence, good temper, unquestioning obedience are all necessary to complete success. In the best hospitals her work will be carefully supervised by the competent sisters, and the practical training which she receives in the wards will be supplemented by lectures on the work, conduct and promise of efficiency will be submitted to the Matron at regular intervals. She will aim at experience in the nursing of men and women and children in medical and surgical work and as far as opportunity allows, in a gynaecological or other specialty. As she shows herself fitted for greater responsibility it will be given to her gradually, but always under a skilled inspection. She will be periodically examined in the subject in which she has been taught in the end of her engagements. If her ability and conduct are considered satisfactory, and she has passed the required examinations, she will receive the certificate of the hospitals. She should be considered as a qualified nurse.

Wage Differentials

A rough idea about the variation in remuneration prevailing in various hospitals can be obtained from the following table 4.3. The table also provides information about nurses with degree and diploma.

Table 4.3

Sl No.	*Category*	*Government Hospitals (US $)*	*Private Hospitals (US $)*	*Clinics (US $)*
1.	B.Sc nurses	1200–1500	800–1250	N.A
2.	General nurses	650–1000	500–800	300–400

There exist vast differences in the wages of nurses in the government and private hospitals.

Most of the nurses working here have crossed the age of 30 years. They migrate mainly from states such as Maharashtra, Tamilnadu, Kerala and Delhi. After acquiring initial experience in those states, they emigrate for better prospects. About 70 percent nurses stay with their families. Those who are married bring their husbands on visit or free visa after taking up the job. Subsequently he finds a job and settles here.

Working Hours

Though the regular duty hours are for 10 hours, it may extend up to 12 hours depending upon the requirement of patient or doctors.

There are two shifts in duty, namely day and night.

Terms and Conditions of Nurses with the Ministry of Health

Following are the terms and conditions of employment contract of nurses who are working with the Ministry of Health.

Salary

The salary includes permissible inducement or social allowance, but does not include other allowances for which an employee may be eligible depending upon the nature of the duty. For example, car allowance or transport allowance, telephone allowance, call allowance, overtime allowance and uniform allowance come under this category.

Advance Salary

The new recruits from abroad are paid, immediately on their arrival, an amount equal to fifteen days basic salary so as to help them to settle down till they receives their first salary.

The advance salary paid is deducted from the monthly salary in three equal installments.

Gratuity

It is computed at the rate of 2.5 days salary for every month of completed service. The salary is inclusive of basic pay and inducement as well as social allowance.

In other words, one month's extra salary will be paid to the employee at the end of December, every year.

Transportation

Free air ticket is provided for the employee from the beginning till the end of contract of employement. Taxi or train fare are payable from home-town to the airport or between inter-connecting terminals ie, domestic to international or vice versa. Air port tax, paid, if any, on embarkation is be reimbursed.

Air-Cargo

The nurses are allowed to air-cargo their personal belongings, up to a maximum of 75 kg, from the beginning till the end of service.

Housing

The nurses are provided sharing accommodation, free of charge in most of the cases. For example, nurses employed with ministry can have admission in a nurses hostel known as Rufaidah Residence located in the vicinity of Salmaniya Medical Complex, or other government accommodation located at Muharraq, Jiddhaffs, or Riffa. When all these options are not possible MOH arranges hired accommodation.

Essential Documents

Before taking up a job, nurses might have provided all information to the recruiting agents so as to qualify in the interview. Once again, after joining, personal information are collected through the authorities.

Problems Faced by Nurses

Although the number of women engaged in nursing the sick is probably greater than in any other profession except that of teaching, lot of ignorance prevails with regard not only to the life and training of nurses but also with regard to the profession.

Several mistaken beliefs are commonly held in this country, that nursing was unknown area before the Christian era. Another is that there was never a nurse worthy of the name before the Crimean war, when the immortal Florence Nightingale rose like a resplendent star, bringing light and hope to her stricken countrymen and showing the way to the hundreds of women who have since essayed to follow her bright example.

It is true that the teaching and example of Christ gave great example to all philanthropic endeavors, the care of the sick more specially the sick poor has ever been emphasised from then onwards.

During the middle ages, the treatment of the sick was primarily in the hands of religious communities. In England, after the Reformation and suppression of the monasteries in the reign of Henry VIII, the sick received but little care. Formerly caring of the sick was attached to the religious houses which had reopened with a staff of layman or laywomen.

Nursing did not improve in the seventeenth and eighteenth centuries. Its practice fell largely into the hands of women of low class, as did that of medicine and surgery into the hands of the barber-surgeon. There were a few devoted nurses as there were some notable doctors.

Miss Nightingale, a highly educated woman of good social position, had all her life been drawn to care for the sick and wounded. She had seized every opportunity to learn all that she could about the laws of health and the causes of disease, as well as how to carry out the practical work of nursing. She was not the only Englishwoman whose heart was filled with a wish to redeem nursing from its degraded position.

Miss Nightingale's forceful character, her determination, her knowledge of the world, and her social position all combined to crown her efforts with success when the Crimean War gave her the great opportunity which she so promptly seized. Her commanding genius and her truly remarkable foresight led her when the war was over, to found the profession of scientific nursing. She realized that it was not the devotion, which was lacking, but the knowledge and hence the foundation of the School of Nursing at St. Thomas' Hospital, where women of a better class than were formerly employed might be taught both its theory and practice.

Problems Faced by Women Nurses

In nursing as in all other branches of women's labour the question of the effect of marriage upon work is very important and difficult one. In its general aspect it lies at the very heart of the whole question of the working women.

The general need of society at the present day is that the most healthy and well –trained young men and women, should be induced to found families and public authorities by this bar put on the trained woman, are doing their best to hinder marriage.

The nursing profession should attract women of good average capacity, general education and good health. Above all do they need public spirit, which will make them anxious to maintain and improve the excellent position medical women have so far obtained. It is very widely interesting life, bringing those who adopt it out of the study into direct touch with human affairs.

The course of study includes the passing of a Professional Preliminary Examination or Matriculation, followed by two years' mechanical work, and two years' hospital practice.

All fully trained nurses start with the same course of training, namely probationers in hospitals.

A short description, by an expert, of each branch of the work open to a nurse when she has completed her general training. There should be proper accommodation, comfortable cubicles or separate bedrooms and a nurse's sitting room.

There should be sufficient food properly served in a room and not eaten in bathrooms or on the staircase.

At present there is no law to protect a nurse from being put on 'night duty' when she has already worked in the day and there is no compensation for a nurse whose health has been permanently injured as a result of nursing others.

The most crying abuse which needs reforming is that of the long hours on duty, which in many hospitals still amount to an average of seventy-three to eighty hours in a week and in some cases even more. If it is realised that in a busy hospital the nurse on duty rarely sits down, and that she is working with her brain as well as with all the muscles of her body, no one can deny that these hours are a disgrace to the country, which prides itself on excellence of its voluntary hospital system.

Despite the hard work, the inadequate pay and the life of sacrifice which must be practiced by a nurse, her profession remains as one of the happiest. The joy of service assisting lives stricken by poverty, sickness and suffering are all hers.

Various Types of Nursing Jobs

A hospital nursing staff falls into two categories. The first category that contains the probationers in training is described Under the General survey of Nursing. The first step after this training is to take the post of a staff nurse. This is usually held for a short time only, for the purpose of gaining experience and learning something of Sister' duties. The Staff Nurse is expected to exercise some supervision over the probationers and to assist the ward sister in their practical training. In the absence of the Ward sisters she will be responsible for the care of the patients.

A ward sister's post is usually considered as the most enviable in the profession. She has considerable responsibility and requires great tact and sympathy in order that she may deal rightly and justly with all under her charge. The patients must be her first care and she must carry out the orders of the medical officers faithfully and intelligently. She must be gentle but firm, cheerful, punctual herself and insisting on the punctuality among others. She must constantly superintend and assist in the practical nursing of the patients seizing every opportunity for teaching the nurses in her ward. Her influence over both patients and nurses is far reaching and should be carefully exercised. Her words and her example may be remembered long after she had ceased her work. She will be held responsible for the cleanliness and order of her ward and for the care of the appliances, utensils and other linen and for the economical use of the ward stores. Her work in many respects resembles that of a mother of a large household, for the sick people, even grown men and women are very much like children in their helplessness and dependence on her. It should bring out all her most womanly qualities.

The next step is probably to a night sister's post. In most hospitals it is that of a senior sister, who is in charge of the patients and of the nursing at night, this work is interesting and the experience is valuable, the salary is slightly higher than that of the ward sister. As a home sister or Assistant Matron the nurse gains her experience of administrative work. There is at present a great lack of systematic training in duties which fall to a Matron. She gains her experience in administrative work. This is to present a great lack of systematic training in the duties which fall to a Matron and such posts are eagerly sought after by any one ambitious to become Matrons or Lady Superintendent. The positions and work of a Matron varies very much according to the size of the hospitals, which may be a small cottage hospital with one probationer, or a large general hospital with two or three hundred nurses. One should not take a Matrons position with the idea of leading an easy life. This is a post with lot of responsibility and anxiety. The worries are inseparable from the position and the salary rarely adequate.

The matron of a large hospital must superintend the catering and other domestic departments as well as the work in the wards and the trashing of the probationers. She must study not only the welfare of the patients and of the hospital but also that of the nursing staff. She must learn now not only the names and faces of her subordinates and pupils but also their characters and their strong points along with their weakness. She must be prepared to spend lot of time in patching up small difficulties which may arise and in making all the wheels run smoothly. She must also be prepared to be misunderstood and to bear the brunt of the blunders and mistakes which must inevitably be made where so many of the workers are totally inexperienced pupils. It is often rendered very happy by the confidence and affection which she receives from her colleagues and from successive generations.

Depending upon the type of contract nurses are provided with the bachelor or family accommodation. Most of them reported that when they reached Bahrain for the first time the representative of the Ministry of Health was waiting to receive them at the airport. For those who are appointed with Ministry of Health, accommodation is generally arranged in Rufaedah Nurse's Hostel. The accommodation comprises all the required facilities such as drinking water, electricity, essential furniture, toilet, air conditioner, fridge and the required safety measures including locks.

The cases which are serious are referred to Salmania Medical Complex. Otherwise ordinary cases are handled by Health Centers. Any way, medical coverage is paid as per the terms of contract. For that, it is required to open a medical file at the nearest Health Center.

Nurses with the Ministry were in praises for the Government. They are paid Settling –in –allowance or advance payment of half month salary as the case may be, from the cash section of the Ministry. It is mandatory to undergo one more medical exam at the Medical Commission located at Al-Razi Health Center, though the migrant might have undergone the same in the home country.

Nursing in private homes and cooperative's

Institution's nurses comprise those who work for private institutes and those who belong to a nurses institute, attached to a hospital. Such a nurse is paid a salary depending upon the mutual agreement between both the parties. It was observed that in some cases about $ 800 was the salary per month. She does private work, being sent to the patients by the institute to which she belongs, the fees are not hers but are paid to the institute. In the intervals between her cases she is housed and boarded and in some few cases she receives a percentage of the money she earns. In some cases she receives as little as $300 per month.

About the independent private nurse there is little to say. She has a poor chance unless she has several doctors who have personal interest in her. If she does not have private income or home of her own, it is not advisable for a nurse to adopt this kind of work. The reasons are high and uncertain employment. This manner of working is suitable only for those who are not entirely dependent on their earnings. There are many who opt it, but the rent for a room is difficult to pay when work is scarce. In addition to that there is the cost of maintenance. There are very few independent private nurses generally applying to nursing homes and private institutions for supplementary cases and in return, she usually pays up the Dinar or in the money she earns, the home or institute acting as an agent on obtaining work for her.

The co-operative system is the most popular and also the most satisfactory for the private nurse. She should depend upon a well known agency that finds the work for her. The advantage of the system is:

1st The nurse takes her own earning

2nd She is protected by the regulation of the agency

3rd Only fully qualified and certified nurses are sent out by these agencies, which do not engage the half trained persons or the failures.

It is important for a nurse wishing to join co-operative to choose a well-recognized agency. Many nurses complain that they do not get sufficient work and their expenses between their cases are therefore, heavy as they are not entirely on themselves. The problem of the nurse employed at a private nursing home is a complex one. Unfortunately her good or ill fortune depends entirely on her employees business. If the home is a flourishing one, the nurse may possibly be offered a fair salary and some amount of comfort. Usually the small, struggling, private homes demand hard work but offer minimum salary and little or no comfort. Even the large and well established homes the difficulties of nurses are not considered. Timings of duty are very uncertain and rarely fixed, the accommodation is bad, the food often insufficient and badly cooked. It is practically impossible for the very small home to give justice to the nurses. It is a disgrace to the nation that this section of women workers is sweated to such an extent.

It is generally agreed that the poor Law Infirmaries are as a rule understaffed with nurses. In some places where often very inadequate provision is made for the efficient nursing of the sick, it is felt that and this against especially in the provision to, made for the efficient nursing of the sick. In many other countries it is also felt that especially in the rural institutions that the status of the Matron or the Superintendent Nurse is not sufficiently defined as being head of and responsible for the nursing staff. This vague and ill-defined position is often the cause of problems in the nursing in smaller workhouse infirmaries and prevents the most suitable nurses from undertaking these important posts. However, the case of Kingdom is reported to be much better in this regard.

In all branches of nursing profession we want the best type of woman to apply for training. But many talented shun to join the profession even today owing to various reasons. Poor law, the floating of scams related to patients and often associated with the failures of life. There are many problems to be coped with and difficulties to be overcome, but at the same time there is much good work to be done. Promising openings arise only for the most efficient.

The drawbacks of nursing, so as to all other branches of hospital work, are the long hours on duty which amount to about sixty-four hours day duty per week or seventy two hours night duty. The engrossing nature of the work as a nurse always requires strict discipline when inside the hospital whether on or off duty. What is constantly apparent to those who work in specialised hospitals is the lack of organisation in the nursing profession in Kingdom unlike the case of India. Another saddening fact is that there is at present no uniform standard of training for them.

Consequently different categories of nurses seek entry into the labour market. There are nurses who receive certificate after three years spent in a small hospital with a very limited number of cases. Or certificate might have been obtained after acquiring experience in a larger institution where the standard of nursing is low. There are cases in which certificates are acquired as a highly trained nurse, has perhaps spent four years in one of the most modern and well equipped hospitals.

At the same time, as the freedom for organised trade union movement and the expression of freedom of opinion is granted by the government in 2002 there are no attempts to dissuade nurses from organising or joining other movements for the improvement of conditions of labour among women. It is beneficial for those women who prefer leading a solitary life to a community life, especially those without home ties, may reckon on healthy accommodation, good food, regulated hours, and on the whole favourable conditions in their work.

Home Nursing

Nursing in schools and nurses as inspectors can also be seen in Bahrain though unlike western countries the Prison nursing is not popular among women. Many women are into the field of midwifery. All through the ages it has been done by women until early in the nineteenth century. In many countries, it gradually became customary for men-doctors to attend such cases. Apart from this, the work of midwifery has never been in the hands of men except when the abnormal cases have required the assistance of a doctor with the knowledge of anatomy and medical assisted delivery.

Those female nurses who had earlier migrated to UK and re-migrated to Bahrain threw some light on working condition of nurses in other countries. This is working among people in their own homes and is a valuable experience to those who are interested in dealing with the social problems of the day. The largest institution of this kind of work in Queen Victoria Jubilee Institute for Nurses incorporated by Royal Charter in 1889, to which are affiliated the majority of the District Nursing Association in the United Kingdom. In addition to full hospital training, the Council of the institute require that any of nurse desiring to be enrolled must have six years experience as a nurse in nursing the sick in their own homes under the supervision and tuition of a superintendent. This experience is for the purpose of enabling the candidate to learn to adapt her nursing skill to the altered conditions as she finds in the ordinary working, and home and also to show her how the friends and relations of patients can be educated to supplement the skilled services rendered by the nurse during her visits. It is difficult at first for the one accustomed to the constant attention and the presence of every appliance, as provided in the wards of a hospital or infirmary, to realize that even an acute and critical case can be adequately attended with a trained nurse being always at hand. During the interaction with nurses, these and many other difficulties are explained and it is shown how the orders of the medical men can be carried out with the required safety, even in the absence of the trained nurse.

Nurses with Defense Force

Interaction with respondents brought out the fact that many Indian women are employed with Bahrain Defense

Force Hospital and are highly paid when compared to existing wage-rate. There are senior nurses who draw a minimum salary valued between $2000 and $3000. Most of them have been working there for past several years and are married and settled. Some of their spouses are also employed with defense. Other than women working as defense nurses, those working with medical complex, hospitals, clinics and medical centers are spinsters.

There are other Paramedical Courses such as dentistry, physiotherapy which need to be discussed here.

Dentistry

The next field having less representation of females is dentistry. Dentists include those with BDS and MDS degrees. However these days dentists who qualify from U.K or America are considered to be eminent whereas those with Egyptian degrees are not considered to be of high standard. Often American doctors are preferred to Indian dentists where are as they are considered to be far superior than Egyptians. In short, they enjoy a place in between. In this field too Indian females are very limited in number.

Physiotherapy

It is another field coming under paramedical courses in which women outnumber men. The number of Indian Physiotherapists are increasing over the years as revealed by many respondents. However, many migrant women expressed reluctance to educate their girl children as physiotherapists saying that technically speaking physiotherapy can be considered as a highly –paid massage.

Engineering\Architecture

In fields such as engineering and architecture, large number of Indians are there, though females are less in number, as they can not cope up with the stress and strain which an industrial job demands. Indian engineers are employed in various fields such as project managers, quality surveyor, Business Development manager, General Manager and Vice President. It has been observed that few single women engineers who are employed now are hesitant to continue their profession after marriage as they expressed doubts whether they can properly take care of their children while devoting attention to their official responsibilities.

Though it was known that there were limited number of women engineers, could not be known about any Indian women Architects. It transpired that one Indian architect whose daughter was acquiring an architect degree in Kerala was planning to seek employment in Bahrain as family is settled there. The salary range of fresh engineers varied from $ 850 to $1000 and experienced varied between $1500 and above.

The study brought out the fact that discrimination in the labour market exists in professionals and in the country as a whole. In all professions racial discrimination exists in the salary structure. For the same job, candidates with the same qualification, local candidates would fetch in almost double wages while a white citizen will fetch in thrice or four times salary than an Indian. The total emoluments paid to different employees vary considerably. The same discrimination is visible in the rentals, transportation and other amenities provided to them. It has to be noted that in all foreign countries the same kind of racial discrimination exists. For eg, a graduate engineer with 4 to 5 years experience generally receives $1500, a Bahraini engineer will easily receive $2000 or $2500 or even more. In the case of American or Englishman the amount shoots up to $4000 or more. The same discrimination is visible in other facilities provided by the firm. The total perks and allowances received by a person with same degree, knowledge or experience vary considerably, only on the basis of the migrant's citizenship.

Massage

This works demands a healthy body and cheerful mind, a love of the work, endurance and much tact in dealing with nervous cases for which this form of treatment is found to be beneficial.

It may be undertaken either as a separate profession, or as an additional qualification by trained nurses.

The training must be good and adequate to ensure any success as a masseuse, so great care should be exercised in the choice of a school. The many training school advertised are of varying degrees of efficiency and those prepared to train in a few weeks, or by correspondence only, are obviously unsatisfactory. Dedication and service oriented mentality of Indian nurses are appreciated in general though Egyptians, Philippinos, English, Srilankans, Bengladeshi and Pakistani nurses are there.

While enquiring the reasons behind continuing in job with extremely severe rules and tough contracts, nurses of Kerala origin provided a shocking information. They reported that they do not belong to well to do families and parents have no money to marry them away. The only alternative before them was to acquire a general nursing diploma, secure minimum experience and to attain a job abroad to help their parents to earn money to marry them away. This points towards the existence of the evil system of dowry prevailing in literate Kerala even after the prohibition of it by Supreme Court of India.

Hotel Mistresses

The introduction of women into the hotel industry services is a modern development, although they have been engaged in it longer than is usually known. Certain duties with regards to hotels and entertainment, which had previously been performed by males, were given to women. The country adopts this method to promote tourism and to entertain foreign tourists. The age of women in this field ranges from 25- 45 years. Very rarely ladies continue in this profession after 45 years. There are two shifts such as 3 p.m to 6 p.m and 6p.m – 2 a.m. The salary varies between $240-$320. As they are poorly paid, they end up in earning money by indulging in entertaining tourists to any extent. Accommodation and transportation are provided by the firm.

There are many Indian dancers who take contract for six months and emigrate to Bahrain on six months visiting visas. Their wages are paid in advance by the hotel which comes around $300 per month. There are many Indian men singers who lead the troop while women perform dances locally called as "Mujara". There are criticisms that prostitution flourishes in this field. There are very few Indian women who are in long term association in this field. The work is not attractive due to inadequate holidays.

To sum up, on the whole the life of a hotel Mistresses is not at all healthy. It is suitable one for a woman of average physique, it demands, great activity, with many hours spent out of doors, and whoever undertakes it must be prepared for surprises and difficulties. She finds herself at a place entirely surrounded by men – indeed everything looked at from the male standpoint.

Women Clerks and Secretaries

Women Clerks are employed in the financial services and in industrial sector of the Kingdom. The clerical,receptionist and secretaries posts are dominated by women. Till a decade ago, Indians predominated in these posts along with Srilankans and Philippinos. Over the years more and more Bahraini women dominate over these fields.

The Indian women who are employed as clerical staff are under constant fear that any moment they can be retrenched due to localisation policy.

Many Indian ladies complained of Philippinese ladies who are more entertaining in nature. In some offices immature directors, managers or higher officers harass them in various ways. When requested to specify the nature of harassment, they declined to go into details though they complained about Philippinos women. However they emphasised that mature Arabi bosses or foreign bosses never ill treat ladies. They were praising many Arabi nationals who respect ladies.

A sense of irritation and dissatisfaction is the use engendered between the two sexes. The maintenance of separate staffs of similar status but with different rates of remuneration, enable the department to pay off one against the other, for the existence of a power paid class makes it increasingly difficult for the men clerks to substantiate a claim for better pay themselves.

There is a woman running a typing office in the City who hires out shorthand typists in order to complete the work taken up from various business firms. She employs a staff of fifteen to twenty girls. Similarly a lady emigrant hails from Kerala successfully runs a travel agency in the heart of Bahrain.

A women with deep knowledge of women clerks and secretaries in the City for the past twenty years, says about the poverty of a vast number of girls. Many of them are the chief breadwinners of the family. She knows of a half a dozen of cases of men of forty and a little older who are living on the earnings of their daughters. A man who was interviewed openly admitted that he is dependent on his daughter who is working as a company secretary.

House Maids

Currently, there are millions of women workers, mostly house maids from the Philippines, Sri Lanka, India and Bangladesh, reportedly working under appalling conditions in several countries of the world, primarily in Middle Eastern countries, including Saudi Arabia, Kuwait, the United Arab Emirates, Bahrain and Oman. In the past, Middle Eastern countries have resisted attempts to open themselves to U.N. scrutiny.

While media reports in recent periods have focused on extreme cases of abuse of domestic maids, the study focuses on the 'more normal' daily work environment and exploitation of these workers, and the lack of adequate international instruments to safeguard these women.

There are lot of girls working as house maids in Bahrain. There are complaints that some of them are not treated properly by their masters. There is no timing or schedule for their work. They used to work early morning 4.30a.m to mid night. Many of them are not getting enough time to sleep or time for personal hygiene.

They are being paid on an average of US $ 130 to US $ 275 per month. Mostly their contract is for two years. And after the end of their contract period they get the benefit of return Air Ticket to their home country. The common age group of house maids are from 25 to 50 years.

Foreign domestic maids in many of Asian countries are not permitted to change jobs within two years of an employment contract. In some countries, for example, Singapore, migrant women are prohibited from marrying local citizens. They are not allowed to raise a family, and to confirm that they have to undergo six-monthly pregnancy tests, as indicated in the survey.

Fields Marked by less Female Representation

The number of migrant women in the civil service is practically nil. The claim that women should be allowed to enter not only the lower but the higher branches if the Civil service is being freely made at the present time. As the country promotes the policy of localisation, there is no scope for migrant women in this field. It is generally felt that the posts in which the holder has to execute the judgment and to decide on administrative matters should be open to women as well as to men.

The educated mass of migrant women whose number is fast multiplying are emerging as new social force all over the world.

The following departments are important administrative departments of any country

The Local Government Boards

The Board of Trade

Labor Exchanges

Board of Education

Nátional Education Board

The National Health Insurance Commissions.

While enquiring about the areas in which hardly any women migrant works, the respondents were requested to answer the following questions, pertaining to migrants from India.

Whether any Indian migrant woman is working in local government boards?

Yes, though limited in number now. Previously they were working in large numbers at various offices of Bahrain and Dubai. They were not employed in more conservative countries like Saudi Arabia. Recently almost all Middle East countries adopted the policy of localisation and as a result very few emigrants are working in this department now.

Whether any Indian emigrant woman is working in the board of trade?

Indian migrant women are not freshly appointed due to above mentioned reasons.

Whether any Indian emigrant woman is working in labour exchanges?

No – in labour exchanges localisation has been done completely.

Whether any Indian emigrant woman is working in board of education?

Very few.

Whether any Indian emigrant woman is working international education board?

Not at all.

Whether any Indian emigrant woman is working in the board of agriculture and fisheries?

No.

Whether any Indian emigrant woman is working in the national health insurance commissions?

Yes- presently also women are working in these departments.

Whether any Indian emigrant woman is working in general post office?

No- this field is hundred percent localised and no expatriate women are working.

In Bahrain, women are well represented in the private sector, with a quarter of employees being female. However in some professions, such a journalism, the figure is much lower with few women reporters.

Bahrain is a country where employment law guarantees women the same rights as men, but takes into account their particular family circumstances. Women are not allowed to work night shifts between 8pm and 7am, except those employed in health care, and certain employment. Jobs which may harm an unborn child are prohibited for women.

Increased economic equality has undoubtedly had its social affects. Women in employment now have to face the burden of child-care and work. The government is aware of these problems, and has encouraged employers to provide crèches and schools to provide after hours clubs. On a more fundamental level work also brings higher expectations and economic equality has the potential to bring about a new relationship between the sexes.

Measures of Improvement

It is a well accepted fact that migration is helpful in providing productive labour and economic improvement for millions of Asian women. Unprotected female migrant workers become an increasing concern, as reported by ILO. From a gender perspective, women should have equal opportunities in immigration and emigration policies and access to international labour markets, their status as migrants or non-nationals, and as workers in a gender-segregated labour markets, makes them particularly vulnerable to various forms of discrimination in the labour market.

ILO has came out with cases of domestic servants who underwent maltreatment, sexual harassment and extra work load. It was noted that extra burden of work was indication of their stressful life. Unable to bear up these tensions some of them were compelled to leave the country before completing the contracts.

Socio-cultural attitudes and perceptions concerning the role and status of women in family, society and work place should undergo change. Gender biases not easily amenable to direct policy intervention.

While the recorded data refers to legal labour migration, and only the part officially recorded as overseas employment migration, it does not cover women leaving a country legally for reasons other than work (for tourism or education) but end up in fact working at the destination. Nor does the data cover those leaving a country illegally to work in other countries. Attempts should be done to tackle the situation.

Approximately 100,000 Indian women are reported to be working in the Middle East. Though the ban on migrant women workers was lifted in Bangladesh only in 1991, Bangladeshi women are also working as domestic labour not only in India and Pakistan, but also in Middle East.

Asian women are now the fastest growing category of international migrant workers and need special protection since, as migrants and non-national workers, they are particularly vulnerable to various forms of discrimination, exploitation and abuse. The effectiveness of policy measures to improve the migrant women's situation by labour-exporting countries is minimal if legislation and labour standards are poor in receiving countries.

Several complaints were levelled against job-placement agencies. Though they are instrumental in facilitating access to scarce overseas jobs, but are costly. Sometimes the agencies keep the passports of the women or they charge exorbitant fees and provide loans to be paid from future earnings.

Most receiving countries in Asia and the Middle East do not allow the migrant women workers to come with their families, and so the women have to emigrate all alone. The residence permit of these workers is linked to their employment, and subject to restrictions.

Asian female migrant labour supply has been very flexible as they respond quickly to changing labour markets abroad. Often they leave their family and country to become income-earners for their families and important foreign exchange contributors for their countries.

There are certain occupations dominated by female migrants such as domestic workers, helpers in restaurants and hotels. All such jobs are at the bottom of the occupation hierarchy, generally shunned by local women because of low rewards, inferior working conditions and limited job prospects and security.

There are cases in which domestic workers are often paid sub-standard salaries, which are sometimes delayed or withheld; there is no days off, food is inadequate, accommodation unsafe and uncomfortable, medical benefits are denied.

There have been cases of sexual harassment, excessive workload and income-related exploitation. Cases in which a major proportion of their earnings are siphoned off to intermediaries are also not rare.

Female workers in domestic service or entertainment services are particularly vulnerable since they go into individualised work situations involving greater isolation and lower level of social support networks.

The survey also highlights the extent of underemployment of migrant labour in terms of the wastage of higher qualifications acquired by them. Among migrants, it was noticed that by understating qualifications many migrates. For a better income abroad, they under-state their qualifications to get the jobs. In the host countries they cannot shift jobs to move to a higher skilled category, but those with higher skills may end up in lower jobs - nurses for example, being forced into domestic service.

While Asian sending countries have played an active role in promoting labour exports, in the final analysis it is more a demand-driven rather than supply-driven phenomenon. The demand from receiving countries for female migrants - domestic workers, nurses or teachers - is more stable than for construction workers. The female migrants are a more reliable source of foreign exchange remittances.

Due to varied reasons as cited below, sending countries have now come under increasing pressure to protect their workers abroad.

But with more sending countries entering the labour export market, there is competition among them while receiving countries have wider choices and cheaper sources of labour.

Many Asian countries have developed restrictions on overseas employment - partly to keep certain skilled workers at home and partly to protect vulnerable workers from exploitation abroad.

But governments in imposing restrictions have had to be careful to ensure that they do not end up motivating women and men to use illegal channels for emigration.

Though there are reports that sexual harassment in workplaces has increased considerably over the years, however, drawing a true picture of sexual harassment in the workplace is difficult. Factors including fear of retaliation, or of losing desperately needed income, or feelings of shame restricts women from complaining against sexual harassments. So the number of cases reported are extremely limited.

The victims of sexual harassment are many. Young women and men in education and training institutions are part of it. The domestic workers, workers with little job security, women in male-dominated occupations, or in situations where a large number of women are supervised by small number of men also undergo sexual harassment. But it seems the domestic workers are very vulnerable to sexual harassment due to high degree of subordination between the worker and employer. It is also due to the fact that domestic services are often excluded from protective labour legislation. Further, the services of a domestic servant can be terminated with immediate effect. Although highly vulnerable to sexual and other violence, but circumstances including isolation, long working hours and lack of social contact mean that few took action.

As the migrants lack support from local community, and may be more afraid of reporting harassment. Further, their numbers are increasing. The export of women workers is being encouraged by many governments. The increased number of female migration is evident from the case of India.

The problems of out migrating workers in general and emigrants in particular should be studied by giving special emphasis to the workers who belong to inferior sectors. The possibilities of educating potential migrants on the conditions of work abroad, on the provisions of their contract, and in Arabic should be taken care of. This contract is often incomprehensible to the migrant worker, and changes are often made to suit the employer.

Moreover, migrant workers rarely receive any copies of their contracts. The contracts signed in India are rendered invalid in the country of work since the law does not recognize any of the provisions stipulated therein. Consequently, workers' salaries, nature of work, benefits and vacation are reduced to the lower in blue collar jobs. Sometimes, the provisions are totally removed, making it more difficult for migrants to claim benefits or file a complaint when disputes eventually arise. Some domestic workers are also required by their employers to submit their travel documents to ensure that they do not run away. While employers are required to register their workers, they often wilfully neglect such obligations in order to harass, or extort money from, their employees when they need to renew their working permits.

Bibliography

1. Abdullan T and Zeidstein S, 1978, "Finding ways to learn about Rural women: Experiences from a pilot project in Bangladesh", Sociologica Ruralis, 18 (2/3): 138 –176.
2. Adams C and Winston K., 1980 Mothers at work, Public policies in the United States, Sweden and China, Longmans, New York.
3. Anker R and knowles J., 1978, "A micro analysis of female labour force participation in Kenya," Population and Employment Working paper 62, ILO Geneva
4. Ardener S, ed, 1979, Defining Females. The nature of women in society, Croom Helm, London
5. Asian and Pacific Centre for Women and Development, 1980 Notes on data collection with special reference to women, APCWD, Bangkok.
6. Banerjee N, 1979 "Indian Women and the Urban Labour.
7. Bangladesh Economics Association, 1977, Role of Women in Socio-Economic Development in Bangladesh, BEA, Dacca.
8. Beechey V, 1978 "Women and production: A critical analysis of some sociological theories of women's work," in Feminism and Materialism, eds, A Kuhn and A Wolpe, Routleedges and Kegan Paul, London.
9. Bengelsdorf C and Hageman a., 1978, "Emerging from Under development: women and work in Cuba," Race and clas, 19(4): 345 – 60
10. Blacker J., 1977, 'A criticque of the International Definitions of Economic Activity and Their Applicabilty in Population.

11. Chaney, E., 1973, 'Women and Population: some Key Policy, research and Action Isues,' in Populations and Politics, ed. R. Clinton, Lexington Books, Lexington.

12. Schmin, and Chaney, E., 1976," Women and Modernization: Access to tools," in Sex and Class in Latin America, eds. J Nash and H. Safa, Praeger, New York.

13. Sida, 1974, women in Developing Countries: Case Studies in Six Countries, Swedish International Development Authority, Stockholm.

14. Ward, B., 1970, "Women and technology in developing countries," Impact of Science on Society, 20: 1-20.

15. Wilensky, H., 1968, 'Women's Work: Economic Growth, Ideology Structure," Industrial Relations, 7(3): 235-48.

16. Adikson, Judith a (1981). Women of school administration: a review of the research. Review of Educational research, 59(3), 311-343.

17. Baig, Tara Ali (1976) Indians Women Power: Sultan Chand A Sons, Delhi.

18. Betz, ellen l. (1982) need fulfillment in the career development of women. Journal of vocational behaviour, 20(1), 53-66.

19. Bhattacharya, S.K. (1973) a study if value system of different occupational groups. Indian Journal of Social Work, 34(3), 223-230.

20. Bhushan A. and Ahuja M. (1980). Value perfernce patterns of Indian Youths belonging to different sociometric levels. Journal of institute of Educational researchers.

21. Crealock Caral (1987). Sex, vocational sterotypes and fear of success in faculty education – students. Ontario psychologist, 10, 91, 15-19.

22. Dutt, Ramesh Chandra (1984-1909) Civilization and Ancient India. As referred in B.Kuppuswami (1972), Social Change in India, Vikas Pulication: New Delhi.

23. Ferre, Myra M. (1983). The women's movement in the working class. Sex Roles, 9(4), 493-505.

24. Gupta, Sarita; Shah M.A. Beg, M.A. (1982). Education and Socio-economic status as determinants of Indian Women's attitudes towards equality of women. Journal of Social Psychology, 118 (1), 139-140.

25. Harmon, Lenore W. (1981). The life and career plans of young adult college women. A follow-up study. Journal of Counselling Psychology, 28 (5), 416-427.

26. Harris, Roma, M. (1983) Changing women's self-perceptions; Impact of Psychology of Women course. Psychological Reports, 52 (1), 314.

27. Hate, Chandrakala A.E. (1969). Changing Status of Women in Post-Independence India. Bombay: Allied Publications.

28. Higgins, Patricia J. (1985). Women in the Islamic Republic of Iran: Legal, Social and ideological changes. Signs, 10(3), 477-494.

29. Kalia, Narendra N. (1985). Sexism as a social problem. Social Change, 15 (4), 27-30.

30. Kuppuswami, B. (1972). Social changes in India, Vikas Publication, Delhi.

31. Lips, H.W. (1988). Sex and Gender: An introduction, Mountain View, CA: Mayfield.

32. Mittal, V.K. (1965). Personality differences among conservative and progressive ladies. Research Journal of Philosophy and Social Sciences, 2, 124-216.

33. Pandey, Rajendra (1986). Rape crime and victims of rape in free India. The Indian Journal of Social work, 47(2), 417-22.

34. Prager, Karen J. (1986). Identity development age and college experience in women. Journal of Genetic Psychology, 147 (1), 31-36.

35. Prasad, Pramila and Bhushan, L.I. (1984). Perceived role conflict among school teachers. Research in Psychology, 3, 41-48.

36. Premi, M.K. (1982). Population growth and educational development. Population of India. New York: United Nations, New York.

37. Qayyum, S.A. (1978). Women in the Muslim World- A Case Study of Egypt. In Phadnis, U., and Malani, I. (Eds.) Women of the World. Vikas Publishing, New Delhi.

38. Sakhkara, S. (1974). A sample survey of women's opinion and behaviour relating to family life as correlates to educational status. Unpublished Thesis. Nagpur University, Nagpur.

39. Sastry, Nalini (1990). Anxiety, sex role orientation and age: Married women in urban India. The Indian Journal of social work, 51(4), 659-668.

40. Smith, Elsie J. (1981). The working mother: A critique of the research. Journal of Vocational Behaviour, 19(2), 191-211.

41. Verma, Indu (1972). An investigation into expectations and aspirations of unmarried college girl students. Unpublished M.A. Field Work Report, Bhagalpur University, Bhagalpur.

42. Yogev, Sara (1982). Are professional women over worked? Objective versus subjective perception of role loads. Journal of Occupational Psychology, 55 (3), 165-169.

43. Munasinghe. (Source: Macro Economic Importance of Middle East Remittances by Chandra Munasinghe. In Channelling and Utilisation of Remittances of Migrant Women Domestic Workers, Colombo: CENWOR, 2001.)

44. Contact CENWOR for additional information.

45. Email: cenwor@slt.lk, cenwor@panlanka.net.

46. Battistella, G. and Paganoni, A. (1992). Philippine Labor Migration. Q.C. Philippines: Scalabrini Migration Center Cohen, Robin. (ed.) (1995). The Cambridge Survey of World Migration. UK: Cambridge University Press. Cohen, Robin. ed.) (1996). Sociology of Migration. Cheltenham: Edward Elgar Publishing Ltd. Cohen, Robin. (ed.) (1996). Theories of Migration. Cheltenham: Edward Elgar Publishing Ltd. Huess, Ralf. (1987) Die Ökonomik der Migration. Universität Köln Leacock, E. and Safa, H., et al. (1986). Women's Work. Masschusetts: Bergin and Garvey Publishers, Inc.Opitz, Peter. (1997) Der Globale Marsch. München: Beck.

Notes

1. Hamilton, N. and Chinchilla, N. 1996. „Global Economic Restructuring and International Migration", International Migration, vol. 34, no. 2 1996, IOM, Geneva[2] Boyd, M. 1996." Family and Personal Networks in International Migration". In The Sociology of Migration. Edited by Robin Cohen. Cheltenham, UK: Edward Elgar Publishing Ltd. 298-301 [3] Barsotti and Lecchini. 1990. in „Philippine Labor Migration" Go, S. and Postrado, L. 1986. „Filipino Contract Worker: Their Families and Communities." In Asian Labor Migration. Edited by F. Arnold and N. Shah. Boulder, Colombo: Westview[5]Arizpe and Aranda,1986. In The Sociology of Migration"(1996), Edited by Cohen, Robin. Company, G. 1995."Women Migrants: from Marginal Subjects to Social Actors." The Cambridge Survey of World Migration". Edited by Robin Cohen. UK: Cambridge University Press. <SUP7< sup>The number of immigrant women working as domestic helpers or in the sex industry is very high at the world rate. There are 200,000 foreign maids in Italy; 25,000 in Spain (1991); 60,000 in UK; 86,000 Sri Lankan women in the Middle East (63,000 in Kuwait) alone, 80,000 Filipina maids in Hongkong and 35,000 in Singapore (Company)

http://www.hinduonnet.com/thehindu/2001/09/13/stories/05132523.htm

http://www.aworc.org/bpfa/gov/escap/27oct02.html

http://web.mit.edu/cis/www/migration/srinivas01.html

http://www.un.org/rights/dpi1772e.html/Country Report (1998): India

http://women3rdworld.about.com/cs/migrantwomen/

http://www.twnside.org.sg/title/height.htm

www.philsol.com

http://www.twnside.org.sg/title/woes-cn.htm

http://www.twnside.org.sg/women.htm

http://migration.ucdavis.edu/mn/entireissues/dec_2000mn.html

http://www.sigi.org/Resource/vaw_bib.htm

http://www.isiswomen.org/pub/wia/wiawcar/india.htm

http://devnetjobs.tripod.com/unifem-delhi.html

http://www.dawn.com/2001/10/03/nat32.htm

http://www.geocities.com/acunu/millennium/ch-11.html

http://www.ips.org/migration/dedios.html

http://www.bahrainbrief.com/english/sep-2001.htm

http://www.google.com/search